When Fore  ⌐st

When Forever Doesn't Last

A Healing Journey Through Divorce

Guy M. Galli, BS

with

David C. Pruden, MS

CFI
Springville, Utah

ISBN 13: 978-1-59955-309-2

Published by CFI, an imprint of Cedar Fort, Inc., 2373 W. 700 S., Springville, UT 84663
Distributed by Cedar Fort, Inc., www.cedarfort.com

LIBRARY OF CONGRESS CATALOGING-IN-PUBLICATION DATA

Galli, Guy Morgan, 1970-
  Surviving divorce in the latter days / Guy M. Galli with David C. Pruden.
    p. cm.
  ISBN 978-1-59955-309-2
  1. Divorce--Religious aspects--Church of Jesus Christ of Latter-day
Saints. 2. Church of Jesus Christ of Latter-day Saints--Doctrines. I.
Pruden, David C. (David Clarke) II. Title.

  BX8643.D58G36 2010
  248.8'46--dc22

2009032739

Cover design by Angela D. Olsen
Cover design © 2010 by Lyle Mortimer
Edited and typeset by Melissa J. Caldwell

Printed in the United States of America

10 9 8 7 6 5 4 3 2 1

Printed on acid-free paper

This book is dedicated to all those brave families who, during their darkest hours, find ways to rise above the conflict, forgive, and live their lives according to a higher law.

Contents

4. Win/Win: A Test of Balance   36

SECTION III: RELATIONSHIP
5. The Art of Listening   44

6. Frequently Asked Questions   51

Introduction

If you are reading these words, it is probably because you or someone close to you is experiencing a mighty life change—a change so prevalent and widespread in our society that it touches all of us either directly or indirectly, yet one that that is not usually spoken of except in hushed voices and neighborhood gossip circles. We are talking about divorce.

If divorce has impacted your life, you are not alone. According to several national statistics,[1] nearly one-half of all marriages in the United States end prematurely in divorce. Other indicators predict an even higher rate.[2] It seems, and the evidence would show, that it is getting harder and harder to find marriages that last "until death do you part," let alone for time and all eternity. Young or old, newlywed or grandparents, and everywhere in between, divorce doesn't pick favorites. For every one of these families a great—and sometimes terrible—change occurs.

As Latter-day Saints, we are not immune to this epidemic. It is estimated that the divorce rate among Latter-day Saints is right around 25 percent[3]—significantly lower than the national average, but still alarming and troubling to local and general Church leadership alike.

For Now We See Through a Glass, Darkly

If you are currently experiencing a divorce—either by choice or by having it thrust upon you—it would be safe to say that you are experiencing a certain amount of shock and distress. It may seem as if the sun has set, and a thick darkness has descended over your life. You may turn to family and friends,

> **Sadness, disappointment, and severe challenge are events in life, not life itself.**
> – Richard G. Scott

and even Church leaders, but their counsel and advice doesn't shed much light on your circumstances. Family members are often feeling the hurt and pain of your separation and divorce themselves and can't be very objective or helpful. Friends who may have also gone through a rough divorce may try to help but often just succeed in spreading their own misconceptions and failures. Many Church leaders, as well-meaning as they are, have not been properly trained in handling the conflict and problems that come from divorce, and may only suggest the name of an attorney that might be able to "help." During this time of chaos and crisis, it is hard to see clearly and keep your wits about you when you are, as Paul said to the Corinthians, looking through a glass, darkly. *When Forever Doesn't Last* is designed to help you dispel the darkness and once again let your light so shine.

Latter-day Divorce

We wish to make one thing clear from the beginning of this work. The authors are neither suggesting nor supporting divorce, nor are they critical of those who have taken this course of action, either by their own decision or the decision of their former spouse. Once the decision to divorce has been made, however, there are many skills and tools that will help parents and children alike manage this change and heal from divorce's often negative effects.

When Forever Doesn't Last is meant to be a practical guide or handbook for those of you experiencing, close to, or feeling the effects of divorce. This book should not be a substitute for seeking your own grief, legal, financial, or spiritual counseling. The authors are neither therapists nor attorneys, and we cannot provide the kind of advice you may require to address your individual circumstances and needs. This book, on the other hand, is the product of our many years of conducting divorce and domestic mediations and conflict resolution coaching.

Mediation

Divorce is still one of those topics not accepted and openly discussed in Church circles, and as a consequence, neither are the available resources. When a leader or marriage counselor concludes that divorce is for the best, a referral to a lawyer or two is about all you are likely to get. Instead, might we, the authors, suggest mediation.

Mediation is a process where a trained and neutral third party helps participants discuss and resolve their differences in a way that meets everyone's needs and preserves a future of continuing relationship. Mediation is almost always a preferred means to separate when you have children. A mediator will use specific techniques to redirect and manage aggression in a way that, in the end, each party has their needs met while making sure that no one gets hurt, or "loses," during the process. Mediators are more than mere referees who make sure that arguments don't escalate and get out of hand. There is a real process and skill to mediation. In our experience, most divorcing parents express concern and doubt whether mediation will help in their particular case, only to be surprised (and grateful) when a resolution is reached. It is a portion of these skills we hope to share with you in this work.

But you will need to do more than merely read this book to get anything meaningful out of it. To borrow an idea from the scriptures, you will need to study it, ponder it, and apply it. You will learn quickly that *When Forever Doesn't Last* is primarily about helping you cope with and grow from your divorce. The information and skills shared in this book will need to permeate your entire being, manifesting in every aspect of your life. It is our hope that your life will take

> **To injure an opponent is to injure yourself. To control aggression without inflicting injury is the Art of Peace.**
> —Morihei Ueshiba, founder of Aikido

on new and deeper meaning, that your wounds will heal quicker, and, maybe for the first time in a long time, peace will fill your life.

When Forever Doesn't Last is also about the creation of a new relationship. We need to be clear that it is not our intent in writing this book to save your marriage. Although these mediation principles and skills can help strengthen any relationship, if you have picked up this book in hopes of learning how to stay together, we would encourage you to seek the assistance of a your bishop, a marriage counselor, or therapist. In writing this book, we assume that you have either separated or are already divorced.

A "Good" Divorce

When Forever Doesn't Last was written to be as helpful and supportive to you and your circle of family and friends as possible. It was not our intent to ignore or pretend that divorce is not devastating and damaging. You may have made mistakes in your relationship, both pre- and post-divorce. You may have said things you didn't really mean and wish you could take back. Maybe you are surrounded by family and friends who mean well but only succeed in urging you to say and do things that don't really help resolve the conflict. Or maybe the pain may have just been too great for you to bear at times, and you lashed out at your children or other loved ones. You may believe that no amount of advice or help can change your "bad" divorce. This is not true! The restorative principles and instruction presented in this guidebook really do work, and if you will internalize them, you are bound to see a difference in your life and the lives of those around you.

Not a Contest

Contrary to what is portrayed in movies and on the news, divorce is not a battle or contest to be won. It is not about getting revenge for all of the horrible things your former spouse did while you were together. When you have children, divorce is little more than a *restructuring* of the family. Instead of living *together* working to raise your children, you now live apart, but your work as parents continues. The titles "husband" and "wife" may only be until the ink dries on the divorce decree, but the most important titles of "father" and "mother" are forever. Nothing can or should interfere with this.

> **Peace is not simply the absence of war. We must wage peace as vigilantly as we wage war.**
> —His Holiness the XIV Dali Lama

But even if divorce is for the best, this restructuring can be a frightening time for you, your former spouse, and your children. Divorce can produce feelings and emotions that range from mild discomfort and annoyance on one end, to a vile hatred and all out war on the other. This chaos and confusion can lead to fear of the future and a defense against a long list of worst-case scenarios. The material presented here is designed to ease this confusion, help you center and refocus your life, and aid in the creation of not only a new relationship with the other parent, but create a better life for you and your children.

No Tricks

Too often the advice you get about dealing with the problems of divorce focuses on your former spouse—your "ex"—and ways to force or trick that person into giving in or otherwise getting your way. *When Forever Doesn't Last* is not a book filled with such shortsighted and manipulative "tricks" to get your former spouse to do or not do something, or to otherwise get your way in a particular situation. Nowhere in these pages is there a promise or even a hint of a quick fix. When it comes to human relationships, there is no such thing. Years of conflict cannot be unraveled in an hour, a day, a week, or even a month, and certainly not in the time it takes you to read this book. This healing is going to take time. Building a new relationship from the rubble of a failed one is difficult and takes great skill and care.

The philosophies, techniques, and skills presented in this book are designed to empower, and therefore *change*, only one person—you. This may come as a surprise, but nowhere in these pages will you find ways to change your former spouse and now co-parent. It simply can't be done. If this was your hope in picking up this book, you have our permission (and encouragement) to put it back on the shelf. The only viewpoints, feelings, thoughts, or actions any of us have any control over are our own. A great deal of time and money is spent (and wasted) trying to control and change someone else. Instead, these same resources, and many others, could be used constructively to improve and sharpen your own skills to make a real and lasting difference in your new life.

A New You

This being said, the practice of these new skills and behaviors will likely invoke suspicion on the part of the other parent. He is going to see a "new" you, and he will have his doubts. He will put you and your new approach to the co-parenting relationship in an effort to determine your sincerity. You may be tempted to throw your hands up at the first sign of this resistance (or the second, third, or fourth), convinced that it just doesn't work. Don't take the bait. Tough it out, and see it through to the end. Remember, this is going to take time.

Don't Be Fooled

Much of what you read will seem like common sense and—yes—even a little basic. There are many simple, practical suggestions and exercises presented here, and you may be tempted to gloss over them and not pay them the attention they deserve. Don't. Masters of any art, whether it is musical, creative, or martial, know the indispensable value of practicing the basics to keep their skills sharp and their foundations sure. The material presented here should become part of your very being if you hope to make any real change. You can't just *imagine* real change. You have to *do* something.

Why Bother?

But why bother? Why take the time to learn how to work cooperatively with your former spouse? You're divorced, after all. You may be saying to yourself (and us), "We couldn't work and communicate effectively when we were married. Why in the world would we want to learn how to talk to each other now?"

> **Relationships that do not end peacefully do not end at all.**
> —Merritt Malloy

The obvious answer: the children. And while that is true, there is another, more personal reason. According the U.S. Department of Health and Human Services, there is a 68 percent to 81 percent chance that you will remarry within five to ten years after your divorce.[4] Whether you believe you will ever find love or open up to anyone again, the consistent numbers speak for themselves—you will move on and find happiness again.

But remarriage is not always the "happily ever after," either. According to several experts, divorce rates for "second marriages with children are much more likely to end in divorce than first marriages,"[5] reaching as high as 67%.[6] According to the American Academy of Matrimonial Lawyers, "Poor communication is often the catalyst for all other marital problems."[7] By working on and improving your communication skills now, with your former spouse and co-parent, you increase the chances of making your next relationship and marriage last.

Organization of Information

We have organized the information in this book in four sections, each one building on the one before it. You may be tempted to skip one or more of these sections, hoping to get the "answers" to your problems and concerns quickly. But just as a child must learn to walk before he can run, the techniques and skills presented here build upon each other. These four sections are: General Preparation, Centering and Balance, Relationship, and finally, Substance.

Preparation

It is of supreme importance that you have a working understanding of conflict and negotiation and their underlying principles. Just as everything was created spiritually before it was created physically, it is crucial you take the time to learn the philosophy and basics of conflict resolution before jumping ahead and calling your former spouse to work things out. Understanding conflict, relationship dynamics, and divorce and its effects will lend you strength and courage, and will help you overcome the "natural man" and help you rise above much of the pettiness usually associated with divorce. This knowledge is necessary if you want to better understand the behavior of others (not to mention your own feelings and actions), bring peace to your life, and proceed with integrity.

Centering and Balance

Centering is the key to making the necessary changes in your life. It makes it possible to harness the powerful energy divorce brings and helps you remain strong and faithful through this trying time. Consider an infant: before he finds his balance, there is little he can do on his own. Once, however, an infant gets his balance, he is able to move, crawl, stand, walk, and finally run and jump. Balance is essential to life. Becoming centered and finding balance in your new life is one of the first steps you will take toward confidence, strength, and peace.

Relationship

Creating and defining a new relationship is the goal of mediation and negotiation. If your relationship with someone is strong enough, you can resolve anything together, no matter how big or devastating. It will be important to see and accept yourself, your children, and your former spouse as they really are, and not as you *wish* they were. This type of self-delusion is counterproductive to creating an effective co-parenting relationship. Seeing your situation for what it is—with all of its strengths and weaknesses—will allow you to change those things you are able to and create lasting peace.

Substance

Finally, as your new life begins to take shape, you can stretch forth your hand and partake of the fruit of your labors. As you read this material for the first time, you might not think it is possible—but it is. In fact, it is more than just possible. You must think of it as essential—as important as air, food, or water. Imagine it, create it in your mind, and then watch as a new, more peaceful life emerges from the ashes of your old one.

Domestic Violence

A word of caution here: if, during your marriage or separation, you or your children have been victims of domestic violence, it is our strongest suggestion that you call or make an appointment to speak to a counselor or victim's advocate to get help moving forward in safety. If you have been a victim of abuse, the very thought of interacting with your former spouse may invoke feelings of panic and nausea, and in many cases, mediation—meeting face-to-face—may not be appropriate. However, many court-appointed mediators are now specifically trained to handle matters where abuse has occurred. Seek out these professionals if you feel that you must proceed with caution—the arrangements, schedules, and interactions can be modified to meet your individual needs and provide you with the distance and safety you require.

When Forever Doesn't Last is a book about change. The skills and philosophy presented here are for you—not the other parent. There is no quick fix, and you may not get all you want or think you are entitled to, but on that journey toward a peaceful end, these principles can bring order out of chaos, give direction when lost, and help heal the wounds of conflict that divorce inflicts on parents and children. It is with this hope that we present this work to you.

NOTES

1. U.S. National Center for Health Statistics, 1994–2004; U.S. Department of Health and Human Services, CDC, updated 2009; U.S. Census Bureau.

2. John Gottman, *What Predicts Divorce: The Relationship Between Marital*

Processes and Marital Outcomes (Hillsdale, New Jersey: Lawrence Erlbaum Associates, 1994), quoted in Daniel Goldman's groundbreaking work, *Emotional Intelligence* (New York, NY: Bantam Books,1994), 129.

3. Barna Research Group, 1999. "Christians are more likely to experience divorce than are non-Christians," Barna Research Group, 1999-DEC-21, at: http://www.barna.org/cgi-bin/ (This article is no longer available online.)

4. Bramlett, MD and Mosher, WD. "Cohabitation, Marriage, Divorce, and Remarriage in the United States," National Center for Health Statistics, *Vital Health Stat* 23 (22), 2002.

5. J. Wallerstein, J. Lewis, and S. Blakeslee, *The Unexpected Legacy of Divorce* (New York: Herperion, 2000), p.28..

6. Gottman, *What Predicts Divorce*, 2 (see also Figure 1.1).

7. "Making Marriage Last," http://www.aaml.org.

SECTION I

GENERAL PREPARATION

If thou prepare thine heart . . . thou shalt be stedfast, and shalt not fear.

—Job 11:13, 15

1

The New View

Neither do men put new wine into old bottles: else the bottles break, and the wine runneth out, and the bottles perish: but they put new wine into new bottles, and both are preserved. —Matthew 9:17

Divorce brings with it a change in which a "new" you is created. Despite your best efforts, you are not the same person, just divorced. Your identity shifts, your name and title—husband and wife, for example—changes, expectations change, you learn the new vocabulary of the legal system, and the list just goes on and on. Attempting to put this "new" you into the old bottle that was your life before the divorce is a recipe for disaster, similar to the one referenced in Matthew. Whether it was your idea or not, divorce creates a "new" you, a new view and understanding of the world and your place in it, the sum of which cannot "fit" into your pre-divorce bottles. To survive this change, an internal shift needs to take place. Some of these "new" views are presented here.

Conflict

When you hear the word *conflict*, what comes to mind? A disagreement? Tensions over touchy or moral issues? Perhaps you think of a heated debate over the separation of church and state, or protests on the courthouse steps as judges decide whether to allow a prayer at a high school football game. Or is conflict more physical? A fight? War? An international disagreement over land rights? Or maybe hatred between ethnic groups? Civil war?

Most dictionaries would define conflict using words similar to as "a state of open or prolonged fighting." A better dictionary may include a reference to a state of disharmony. This supports the common association of conflict with war: forces in opposition, advancing, and retreating until one is declared the winner.

Though true in some sense, these basic explanations are misleading and should not be exclusively applied to the world of divorce and the struggles encountered with cooperative parenting. In our experience, a better and more complete definition of the type of conflict many separated parents experience involve what we reference as the Four "I's": Interaction, Interdependence, Incompatible goals, and Interference (real or imagined—it makes little difference). Let's explore how these four elements of conflict feed off each other until tiny molehills of misunderstanding erupt into mountains of animosity and malice.

Interaction

Conflict requires an interaction, or connection, between two or more people—direct, indirect, physical, emotional, it doesn't matter. This interaction is necessary to begin and sustain conflict. If one or both sides can withdraw from the argument, or completely terminate the relationship, any conflict will dissolve of its own accord. This kind of separation or withdrawal, however, is harder to accomplish than one might think. If you have children, it cannot be done without severe and long-term psychological and emotional consequences to you and your children. You can't just walk away from your children or the other parent. You also cannot simply avoid the fact that you created children together and have a responsibility and obligation to parent them together. Until it is effectively resolved, the conflict remains, and in many cases it continues simmering on the low heat of silence, just waiting to boil over at the first opportunity.

Interdependence

The second part of our definition of conflict that makes it more useful than Webster's is that the parties in conflict are *inter*dependent. Because this is a crucial point we are making, let's look at the three levels of "dependent" relationships.

The most basic relationship level is *dependence*. In the dependent relationship, one or both sides rely on someone or something else to function and achieve their goals. Be it physical, mental, emotional, or spiritual—their very survival is grounded in the reliance on this outside need or force. An infant has a dependent relationship on the adults in his life for food, shelter, and love. An infant cannot survive on its own. Similarly, many abusive relationships are dependent ones. Victims cannot leave because they think they are dependent and need the "love" and support of their abusers, putting themselves firmly under their control. Dependent adult relationships are typically unhealthy and destructive.

Becoming *independent* is the next rung on the relationship ladder. People in an independent relationship can function, live, and thrive without relying on each other or outside forces for their needs. They are self-sufficient and can function just fine on their own. Divorcing when there are no children and very little real or personal property could result an independent relationship. Neither side needs the other for anything. Each could walk away and conceivably never see or even think of the other again. One important element of the independent relationship is that there are no mutual consequences. One side could go to prison, get remarried, or move to Morocco, and it would not have the slightest effect on the other.

The third, and most evolved and complex level, is the *interdependent* relationship. In this relationship, the two or more sides are independent of each other and *can* function on their own, but choose to work *together* to achieve a greater good. This is where the relationship becomes "greater than the sum of its parts." On a very basic and physical level, children are the result of an interdependent relationship in that two adults joined together to create life where they couldn't otherwise create it on their own. Consequences play a big role in the interdependent definition. Unlike the independent relationship, consequences of one or both sides not fulfilling their part have serious effects on the outcome. Divorcing when there are minor children creates a forced interdependent relationship called cooperative parenting.

Incompatible Goals

Returning to our definition of conflict, the third element of divorce conflict is when both parents have, or think they have, clashing, opposite, or otherwise incompatible goals. Simply put, it doesn't matter whether you are actually at odds with your spouse, so long as it *appears* that you are—that there is not enough to go around, or that only one of you can have your way—you will do anything to not only promote and reach your own goals, but you will also start sabotaging the other parent's needs and wants. This is called a zero-sum game in which for you to win, the other must lose, and vice versa. Any benefit you would gain is cancelled out by the loss of the other—the sum, or result, is zero. It is an "all or nothing" game.

Interference

This last element of domestic conflict is an important one as it gives the conflict the "personal" touch and brings out the worst in people. Not only are your goals seen as incompatible, it seems that your former spouse is deliberately preventing you from reaching them. Defenses are raised, tempers erupt, and the conflict becomes infinitely worse. The other parent's actions are seen as personal attacks, and the real issues may become lost in the battles of this newly declared war. It is interesting to point out that this interference doesn't have to be actual or real. Too often parents just sense or "know" that the other side is going to stall, interfere with, or wreck their chances for reaching their goals, whatever they may be.

To make matters worse, if you anticipate problems, you might be tempted to prevent the other side from ruining your plans. By getting in the first shot, you might think that you can head off the interference that you are sure is about to happen. This, of course, creates the very conflict you were trying to avoid in the first place. Whether it was actually going to happen, when you make that "first move" you are now seen as the aggressor, as the "bad guy," and the your problems—real or just imagined—are now worse.

Good or Bad?

Having just defined conflict as it applies to divorce and co-parenting, we want to say that conflict is not necessarily a bad thing. Seeing conflict as an opportunity will help you feel more comfortable addressing and handling it. In many instances conflict is natural and even necessary to spark and create life—cells divide and break off, and divide again, muscles are torn down only to be built up again bigger and stronger. Conflict has a way of announcing that something in our lives, some part of our relationship, is out of balance or not healthy. Conflict can be a "red flag" that aspects of our lives need to be fixed so that peace can again prevail.

The "negative" energy usually associated with conflict is not always negative at all. This energy is, in fact, just energy. How we perceive it and how we use it determines whether it is a bane or a blessing. Are you doomed to be overtaken and hurt by it, or are you committed to manage and direct this energy to create something for your benefit?

Conflict vs. Contest

Before we proceed, there is a point that must be made when it comes to conflict resolution: conflict is not always a contest. A contest is an event, like a game, with clear, simple rules, objectives, and goals. In a contest, both sides must be willing to play, know that they are playing, and be evenly matched. Sports are excellent examples of contests: football, baseball, wrestling, soccer, and so on. Contests are designed to test and prove skill, and by their nature create both a winner and a loser. Conflict, on the other hand, doesn't need a winner—it needs a resolution.

Divorce is not a contest. Let us repeat: Divorce is NOT a contest. It is not a sporting event. No child dreams of someday growing up and playing in the National Divorce League. There is not a Divorce World Series (although sensational divorces that make the news can resemble one). Though there may be a willingness on both sides to separate and divorce, neither side enjoys spending their life savings and other tangible and emotional resources to "play" the game of divorce. Divorce is a conflict that needs to be identified, addressed, and resolved in a manner that everyone—especially you and your children—can live with.

Court "Contests"

Despite the fact that a divorce is not a game to be won, the courts and legal system have a tendency to turn a divorce into a contest by the words and phrases they use. Divorce quickly changes from a conflict in need of a resolution and a relationship that needs to be redefined and re-created into a contest to be fought out and won. Let us explain. When you file for divorce, the filing is either "contested" or "uncontested"; your identity changes from spouse and parent to "plaintiff" or "defendant" on either side of a "vs."; attorneys are hired to "champion" your cause or your fight in the "arena" of court; and judges are like referees and scorekeepers as they are asked to make decisions and determine fair and foul play. One parent is "awarded" custody, while it is said that the other side "lost" his children. Marital debt is assigned and assumed, and you carefully keep "score" as your real and personal property is divided up.

And let's not forget the "rules" of the game. The volumes of code and statutes are the "rules" you and the court must follow. These are confusing, sometimes contradictory, and anything but clear and simple (if they were, we wouldn't need attorneys and judges to interpret them). Just when you think you finally understand them, the rules change with the annual meeting of state legislators.

As far as your children are concerned, divorce is little more than a restructuring of the family. It is generally unwanted, causing a wide range of uneasy feelings and emotions in their little hearts and minds. If your divorce turns into a fight, your children's lives become terrifying, enough so to make them physically sick to see the two people they love more than anything else in the world hating and hurting each other. The love that once existed between their mom and dad is replaced animosity or, worse, apathy, and many children live the next few years worrying if their own love and relationship with their parents is in this same danger.

Divorce is not a contest or a fight. It is not about who did what to cause the break-up and seeing that they are punished. Divorce is not about "winning." It is about doing what is best for you and your children, negotiating a fair separation and settlement, and learning how to work together as co-parents.

Handling Conflict

Conflict exists everywhere. It always has been, and it always will be. From our infancy and youth, we are all taught ways to deal with conflict, and some are better than others. The society we live in, and even the religious and racial cultures we belong to, shape how we view conflict and the right and wrong way to handle it. At home, at school, at church, in the books we read, the movies we watch—everywhere we turn we are learning about conflict and how we should and shouldn't handle our problems. Some of these instructions are gender specific. Boys are generally more direct in resolving differences, challenging the other boys to a fight at the flagpole after school and slugging it out to the last man standing. Girls, on the other hand, may tend to use verbal or other indirect attacks, like starting a rumor or sharing an embarrassing or damaging secret. Girls prey upon their victims using the weapons of emotional warfare. Boys are taught to get up and dust themselves off, while girls seek out comfort and support from other girls and are given permission and time to begin their healing from the inside. Much of this childhood schooling is ingrained in us today. Think back to your old grade school days. Were you told to just walk away, stand and fight, not take "it," or tell a teacher? How do you handle conflict today?

The Big 5

Although there are hundreds of individual ways to deal with life's everyday problems, there are five general methods or strategies of conflict management. Neither is inherently better than the other, and each has their time and place to be effective and useful. Knowing what they are, however, will give you more options when faced with conflict. These general strategies are avoidance, accommodation, competition, compromise, and collaboration.

Avoidance. Running away, shunning, or staying away from conflict are all forms of this conflict management strategy. Avoidance can be used effectively to change the location or environment of the conflict. Avoiding conflict does not necessarily make one a "coward." The time and place could be all wrong; you might not be sufficiently prepared to confront someone. Used properly, avoidance could give you time to "regroup" and better handle the situation; however, refusing to answer the phone or return voicemails or emails for days or weeks on end only serves to prolong and increase the conflict.

Accommodation. This is where a person gives in to avoid the negative consequences of continuing the "fight." This is the "give-in-and-move-on" approach to issues and items in dispute. Accommodation is a valid and effective way to deal with conflict when the stakes are not that high and the issues not worth fighting over. Sometimes it's just better to give the opposition what they want and be done with it.

Competition. This method is all about getting your way. You'll fight tooth and nail to get what is yours. The bottom line is victory, and you will win at all costs. Competition may be necessary when the stakes are high, or when the consequences affect more than just you.

Compromise. This is when both give in a little to find some acceptable middle ground in which to settle. This means that neither side gets everything they want or need, and each goes away having "lost" something that was important to them. On the other hand, there may not be a great deal of time to find an alternative solution, and your best chance for resolution is in "making a deal." Despite this strategy's obvious flaw, compromise continues to be the conflict resolution tool of choice.

Collaboration. This is the fifth strategy for dealing with conflict, and one that is not generally thought of when presented with conflict. Collaboration is the idea that a new and better solution can be found by working together than by working alone. This idea of collaborating, or working together to create something new and better, is the underlying principle of effective co-parenting. Collaboration is the best way to reach a productive and lasting cooperative parenting agreement and will be the theme throughout most of this book.

Collaboration

Collaboration, as a conflict resolution tool of choice, is not as unnatural as you might think. Whatever you remember from high school biology, nature is not all about cold competition and survival of the fittest. Quite the opposite is true. Nature is filled with examples of collaboration—animals that work together to sense danger and warn one another, or who hunt cooperatively and then share their catch. On a much larger but more basic scale, life as we know it is the result of a special collaboration between the plant world that produces the oxygen we breath, and animal life that converts it into carbon dioxide for our photosynthetic friends. But examples of cooperation and collaboration do not generally make good Hollywood entertainment, and so a harsh, competitive world is portrayed as our "nature."

Society too is filled with examples of collaboration. Take the daily commute on the freeways across America. Every weekday morning and evening millions of workers take to the wide lanes and face the conflict of getting millions of cars in and out of downtown Los Angeles. "Conflict?" you say. Yes. The morning commute fits our definition of conflict. Rush hour is an interaction of people, interdependent on each other to some degree, with incompatible goals of all trying to get to work by 8:00 A.M., and at least perceived interference from the other drivers on the road. Oh, it's a conflict, all right. We can see people in this situation employing any one of the five strategies for dealing with conflict.

Avoidance. There are those who avoid the freeways altogether, finding alternative ways to work—walking, riding a bike, or even working from home. Now, there is nothing wrong with this strategy. At times this is the best way to deal with the early morning commute. Learning of an accident on the 405 while listening to the radio traffic reports might require getting off the freeway and wind your way to work on the surface streets. (Of course, everyone else who heard that report had the same idea and you still face traffic that is backed up for blocks.)

Accommodation. We all know the driver that tap their brakes to make room for and accommodate an entire on-ramp's worth of vehicles to sneak in front of him.

Compromise. The compromiser is a little harder to spot, but he is the driver that lets one car merge in front of him, but then refuses to let another until he needs to merge himself, after which he is generous again, trading favors at sixty-five miles an hour.

Competition. The driver who sees his morning commute as a competition is easy to spot. This is the guy who thinks he owns the road: cutting people off, angry at the world, driving like it is a race, all the while thinking that he somehow "loses" the rush hour game if he lets you merge.

Collaboration. But by and large, most drivers on these busy roads operate using the principles and practice of collaboration. If they didn't, accidents would increase a thousand fold and the freeways would shut down. The collaborator knows that it is in his best interest to see that both of you make it to work safely and as close to on-time as possible. Sometimes they give a little, sometimes they may need to take, and that's okay. Accidents happen, but for the most part the commuters on the freeway make it safely to and from work in collaboration with the other drivers on the road.

Co-Parenting Collaboration

When Forever Doesn't Last is all about collaboration and working together with your former spouse—your children's other parent—and, no, it is not as unnatural as you might think. It may not be easy, but in the end it is the only acceptable and healthy solution. Becoming independent—sure and steady in your own life—is the first step, and the next chapter is dedicated to helping you do just that. Divorce and its aftermath is filled with conflict—forced interaction, shared

> Divorce does not produce "single" parents. Parents produce "single" parents. Divorce produces parents who live in separate houses.
>
> –Thayer & Zimmerman,
> *The Co-Parenting Survival Guide*

goals of raising your children and helping them through this difficult time, and at least perceived interference from the other parent. This type of conflict is best resolved using collaboration, and we are going to show you how this can be done.

The Four Levels of Conflict

In addition to the practical strategies of dealing with conflict, there are ethical considerations when choosing a way to resolve the problems and disputes we face. Many mediators and other experts in the field agree that there are four levels of conflict.

At the *first*, or lowest ethical level, conflict takes place when one is attacked without warning and without provocation. In the criminal world, this could translate into a mugging or any other situation where a victim is innocent of provocation or blame in the attack. This would include any and all crimes against children. The word *tragedy* would best describe the effect of this level of conflict on people.

The *second* level of conflict includes shared blame for the attack. The victim may have provoked or taunted the attacker into choosing her or him. Angry words or accusations may push someone "over the edge" and into a physical confrontation. In the world of relationships, this may translate into the ever popular "he had it coming" scenarios. Names may be called and insults thrown before the attacker "gets even" and attacks.

At the *third* ethical level of conflict, the victim of a crime (provoked or not) turns the tables on the attacker during the course of the conflict, and defeats him, beating him at his own game. To most of us, this level of conflict is almost "romantic" and is seen as the highest level: the attacker gets what's coming to him. Hollywood has made billions of dollars using this "higher" ethical level of conflict. This is the type of conflict resolution that makes for good inspirational blockbusters—the "David" that rises to the challenge and defeats the giant "Goliath," giving him everything (and usually more) than he deserves. This is the underdog story. But as entertaining as it is, and as good as it may feel, this level is not the highest level of conflict resolution. However justified the victim may be in his or her actions, in the end, one or (usually) both are still injured in the fight.

The *fourth*, or highest, level of conflict resolution is at the height of integrity and honor, and the principle upon which mediation is predicated. At this level the conflict is resolved and diverted in a manner in which neither the attacker nor the victim is harmed. At this level, no one gets hurt. To the dedicated mediator and warrior of peace there is no other goal. There may be many opportunities to fight back and defend yourself against the attacks of your former spouse.

You may even be justified and have the means to inflict harm, perhaps in the name of safety and security, and provide an opportunity to show that "what comes around goes around." But when you inflict injury in any of its forms, you play a willing part in perpetuating the conflict, inviting further attack—either now or later, when the "time is right." At this highest level, however, you see that it is the *attack* you want neutralized—not the attacker.

Redirecting Energy

It should come as no surprise to learn that it takes less energy and is safer to divert an attack and neutralize it than to meet it head on and stop it. It is the difference between blocking a strike and blending with it. Let us illustrate with a physical example. Traditional martial arts, like kung fu or karate, teach a wide range of blocks to stop an attack, be it foot or fist, many times clearing the way for an attack of your own. When you attempt to stop an attack by raising your arm to block it, victory goes to the strongest. And even if you are the one who prevails, chances are you will have a bruise as a trophy of your success. Compare the blocking scenario to one in which you step quickly, moving close to your attacker and his clenched fist, and then blending skillfully with the direction of his attack, throwing him off balance (there was nothing to resist the momentum of his attack), allowing you to control what happens next.

If you refuse to strike back in kind, you set a new standard in resolving the conflict and lay down new rules for the engagement. In short, by not reacting to the attack with one of your own, you—not your attacker—are the one in control. By blending, or joining with your attacker, you are free to explore the cause or drive for the attack. By not escalating the attack with one of your own, the clutter begins to clear, a resolution begins to take shape, and a peaceful end to the conflict enters your view.

This fourth level is the fertile soil where you can plant and cultivate the seeds of collaboration. As you will remember, collaboration is the means by which a new and better solution is created by working together toward a common goal. But just like you can't set this book down right now and simply expect to neutralize the next attack that comes your way, it is foolish to think that you can just pick up the phone, call your former spouse, and come up with a solution to months, or perhaps years, of conflict. It is going to take time, and it is going to take something else: negotiation.

Negotiation

What do we mean by "negotiation"? Is it bargaining? Demanding to get your way? Giving in? Calling in a favor? Taking what's yours? Is negotiation upfront? Is it clandestine? Is it right? Is it wrong? Verbal? Physical? Is it open and honest family mediation, or haggling over the sticker price of a used car? Do you need training to negotiate, or can anyone do it? Does it include coercion and threats, or enticements and rewards? None of the above? All of the above? Confused yet? That's okay.

Boiled down, negotiation is a process of getting what you want from someone or something that is, at least to some degree, unwilling to give it to you. Implied in any negotiation is the fact that what you want is valued by the other side, though not always to the same degree or for the same reasons. The process of negotiating is the process of getting what you want from others. Negotiation can be aggressive if force is applied to simply take what you want, or it can employ deception and strategies. Negotiations can be at the table, face-to-face, or by letters and written offers sent back and forth until a resolution is reached.

Every negotiation strategy and style has an appropriate time and place. If you or a loved one's life is in immediate danger, "aggressive" negotiations may be necessary in order to save a life. If you are buying a car, coming in with a low-ball offer and then bargaining back and forth as you approach an agreeable price might be the negotiation style *de jour*.

When we use the use the word *negotiation* in the context of divorce co-parenting, we mean negotiating with integrity. Bargaining, as popular as it is with people and cultures, tends to miss the integrity mark. The philosophies behind bargaining are based on withholding important information from the other side and hiding your true wants and needs. Put generally, bargaining is based on a script of telling lies, or at least hiding or distorting the truth. Though appropriate at a street bazaar or used car lot, bargaining is not recommended if you must maintain any level of relationship for future dealings. In other words, it is not wise to attack, hurt, or cheat someone if you have to deal with them later on. In the world of divorce, this means not doing anything to your children's other parent that may cause them to seek revenge or "fight fire with fire" later. Hurting them physically, mentally, or emotionally should be avoided at all costs. It doesn't matter what happened to bring you to this point. You are still family, and family doesn't do that to each other.

The "Hard or Soft" Trap

A common pitfall most people stumble into when exploring negotiation is the misconception that negotiation is either hard or soft. We have all been faced with the choice of "playing hardball," to protect our interests or to get the job done right, or being seen as "soft" and giving in, setting ourselves up to get walked all over. With only the extreme positions being offered, we tend to be blind to the possibility of finding any middle ground. It is a fool's world to limit yourself to only two choices or two outcomes, neither of which is really that great.

With this hard or soft mentality, there is a tendency to value or rate one style better or worse than the other. Given only two choices, most people will opt to play hardball, choosing to hurt someone else in the process instead of getting hurt themselves. Of course, if asked, it is always "unfortunate" that someone gets hurt, but what other choice do they have? At least one.

Fight or Flight

Four of our five basic strategies for dealing with conflict fall into one of two categories of responses to conflict. These responses are *fight* or *flight*. The fight response employs Competition and Compromise, while flight uses Avoidance and Accommodation. (Our fifth strategy, Collaboration, is a mix between the two, but we'll get to that later.) This fight or flight response to being faced with danger or other forms of conflict is very real and measurable. Our hands begin to shake, our heartbeat picks up the pace, our throats get dry, we can't think clearly, we begin to stammer, and our bodies are filled with a nervous energy that either invigorates us or makes us feel nauseous. This is caused by a surge of adrenaline that is preparing us to either run from the danger or conflict before us, or stay and fight.

But as natural as these instincts are, we are not limited to them. As members of the human race, we all have the ability and agency to choose our response to outside stimuli. To deny this response-*ability* is to deny the power and control over your own life and the peace that could be yours.

Faced with conflict, many people give into this "natural" instinct and limit their responses to either a hard (fight) or soft (flight) reaction. The philosophy upon which this book is based offers a third response to conflict: *flow*.

Flow

The concept of flowing or blending with an attack is foreign to most of us. On the surface it may appear to be a weak or soft means to handle conflict. Do not be deceived. Flow is the principle behind collaboration and effective and long-term conflict resolution. By refusing the "either/or" response to conflict most people expect to receive when going on the offensive, you take control of the situation and begin creating new ideas for reaching a resolution, instead of perpetuating the conflict. There is, however, no "one size fits all" way to effectively handle different types of conflict. To truly be effective and remain safe throughout the confrontation, you will need to know and practice dozens of techniques and have numerous conflict resolution "tools."

Negotiation Toolbox

Just as you cannot build a house using only a hammer, you cannot respond to every conflict in the same way. And just like building a house, building and repairing a relationship requires the use of a wide assortment of conflict resolution "tools."

As we explained earlier, there is no "best" strategy or means of resolving conflict—each has its time and place, though when it comes to cooperative parenting some forms

> **When the only tool you own is a hammer, every problem begins to resemble a nail.**
> —Abraham Maslow

of negotiation produce better results than others. Effective negotiators have any number of negotiation skills, or "tools," to use in any number of situations. These tools include active listening techniques, the use of both closed and open-ended questions, testing possible solutions with "What If" scenarios, establishing a strong BATNA—the list just goes on and on. We will discuss all of these negotiation "tools" later in this book.

Just Do It

For now, though, just take a minute, relax, and reflect on words and philosophies we have just covered. It's a lot to take in. Take a deep breath. You don't have to believe everything we've said just yet. But we would encourage you to look at your divorce—as bitter and ugly as it might be—and begin to see it in a new and more productive light. This is the first step. This is why we have this information here in the first chapter. Take another minute or two and answer the questions below. Be honest with yourself—no one else is going to see your answers—and take notice of your responses. They may tell you more than you think.

1.   In what ways has your divorce been like a contest?
2.   What is your primary response and strategy to conflict?
3.   Do you see conflict as mostly negative? Can you see how it might be a good thing?
4.   Is it good enough to have the problems fixed, or do you feel the need to "fight fire with fire"?
5.   When have you been able to "see" your former spouses' point of view on something you have resisted or fought about?
6.   Are there family and friends in your life that "fuel the fire" of the conflict?

2

The New You

Just as the "new wine" discussed in the New Testament parable can't be put into old bottles, nor can the new philosophies and teachings we have just covered be effectively put into the "old you." You need to make room for these new thoughts and concepts. Actually, you need to make your life a "new bottle" to house this new way of looking at and handling the many facets and elements of your divorce. You need to fashion a new bottle, create a "new you." This chapter is going to help you do just that.

Just Relax

Easier said than done—we know. It is important, however, that you allow yourself (or *make* yourself) live a more relaxed and comfortable lifestyle. Just as you wouldn't go jogging in clothing three sizes too small (no matter how good they look), you can't expect to create a new and better life for you and your children if you are living cramped and uncomfortable.

Divorce is a time of uncertainty and incredible stress. Though some level of anxiety is normal and even healthy as you embark on your new life, there comes a time when you must decide to move on and venture out into the great unknown. Finding time away from the conflict, and even a night away from your children, is crucial to your mental health. Your life should be relaxed and have as few rigid absolutes as possible. Cut yourself some slack. You are not a Superman or Wonder Woman. No one expects you to have it all figured out the moment this change occurs. Try to take life as it comes. Yes, you're tired, you're confused, and you're scared—acknowledge those feelings and emotions, accept them for what they are, but don't let them control your every waking moment. Find some time alone. Join a book club, take a tai chi course—do something for you, and find a way to relax.

Flexibility

Any athlete knows the value of keeping the body flexible. Stretching out before and after every workout keeps the muscles loose and healthy, and lets them develop properly. Flexibility is the key to balance. It helps you to avoid strain and injury. It is no different here. As you embark on your new life, it is important to remain flexible,

Just as flexibility is important to the health and condition of your physical body, being flexible in your life as a co-parent is just as important. This flexibility is gained by prioritizing values and events in your life. It is separating your wants from your needs. It is shedding forever an "entitlement" mentality.

It is true that with the signing of the divorce papers comes a sense of liberation, a sense of freedom and permission for you to go your own way in life. Though this may be true on one level, it is deceiving on others. Let us explain.

When you choose to get married, you give up some of the freedoms you had by being single. Your responsibilities increase and you now have another person's wants and needs to consider, so you may not drop everything and go to Vegas for the weekend. The benefits far outweigh the "loss" of these freedoms, but a trade-off happens nonetheless. When children arrive and become part of your life, more freedoms are "lost." You now have the added responsibility for a child who depends on you for his very life. Now the two of you can't split for Vegas on the weekend without considering the needs of your child. Again, compared to your life before children, this trade for the love, peace, and fulfillment as a parent is worth more than all the riches in the world.

When you divorce, whether you asked for it or not, there is a tendency to believe that those freedoms that were once yours before marriage have been restored to you. As logical as this might sound, nothing could be further from the truth. In fact, when you divorce, you give up even more freedoms. Not only do you have your former

> **Practice "No Matter What"—the ability to choose what we will focus on to make us happy.**
> —M. J. Ryan, *Attitudes of Gratitude*

spouse reminding you of your responsibilities as a parent, but you also have the law or a judge restricting what you can do or even where you can live. Becoming and remaining flexible in your life and attitude will keep you from "snapping in two" or otherwise getting "hurt" as incredible pressure is applied to you and your life.

Falling and Rolling

One of the next skills you must practice and master is learning how to fall safely. Not literally, of course, but how to "fall" when things happen outside of your control and threaten to "knock" you down and how to roll with it without getting injured. Learning how to "fall" properly in divorce and co-parenting negotiations equates to planning scenarios ahead of time. These are the "what if" questions you have to ask yourself, preparing beforehand what you will do and how you will respond if they actually happen. This way you are not caught off guard and forced into saying or doing something that you will regret, or that brings injury to you or your co-parent. It is crucial that you always have a plan.

But what can you plan for? What if your former spouse gets married and moves to Wisconsin (you live in Phoenix), taking the children with her? What if you get an angry call from your co-parent over an unpaid orthodontic bill? What if you have words with each other and the child support checks stop coming? What if you are told not to bother picking up your children this weekend because "they won't be there"? What if you or the co-parent converts to another religion and wants the children to follow suit? What if one of you is injured and special care of the children is necessary? What if your teenager wants to live with his or her other parent now? What if . . . ? What if . . . ? What if . . . ? Always, always, *always* have a plan. Think about it. Plan for it. Prepare yourself for change.

Are You Strong Enough?

Strength training is a critical part of any exercise program. Having a strong back and strong legs will help you develop an immovable stance that will allow you to turn and move correctly, help you maintain your balance, and let you work on other areas of the body safely. Too little strength and you could get hurt; too much strength and you might hurt someone else.

In your life as a divorced co-parent, you must get on with life. There is great strength in finding out who you are again. In many cases, this change in your life provides you an opportunity to reinvent yourself and be whoever you would like to be. In some ways it is a clean slate, a chance to learn and grow in different and better ways. You can choose a different course in life to follow: go back to school and finish that degree, take those art classes, cut and dye your hair, start a new hobby as you follow the beat of a new drum. There is great power and strength to be found in this new identity, and it will come to play later in this book and will be instrumental in your life.

The key, however, to receiving this often disguised blessing hidden in every divorce is deciding to really and truly "divorce" your former spouse. Men and women alike are often caught up in the emotional throws of divorce, seeing it as a contest that must be won at all costs. To an outsider, it appears that they have forgotten what they set out trying to do—divorce, disengage, and separate from each other. They not only need to leave each other, they need to leave each other alone. For many, the divorce is granted, but the fight goes on, and although their marriage was not "until death do you part," their anger and their fight are. These detours can prolong the final divorce and prolong the pain. You must be strong enough not to allow your emotions to control the next few years of your life. Remember, your emotions belong to you, not the other way around. The grief and loss you experience is difficult enough without being burdened with the need to continually punish your former spouse for wrongs inflicted upon you. Let go and focus your precious energies and resources in rebuilding you and your new life.

Speed and Timing

Sometimes survival is all about speed and timing. Divorce is full of surprises, and life comes at you pretty fast. If you are surprised by something your former spouse, the attorneys, or the new stepparent does and you cannot act quickly enough, you may say or do things you will regret later. You must be prepared physically, mentally, and emotionally for any situation that might arise during this unstable time in your life. But being prepared and having a plan for your own life is not enough. You must also have a plan for challenging events in your children's lives, as well as the life of your former spouse. Just as it is important to be flexible—planning for the myriad of "what ifs" that could come your way—it is equally important that you be ready to carry out a plan. Even the smallest hesitation could mean the difference between success and failure in your co-parenting relationship.

A New Vocabulary

The world of divorce can be a frightening place, and part of that fear comes from the new language that is spoken there. People around you appear fluent in this foreign language, casually using words like *plaintiff, defendant, petitioner, respondent, child support, custody, visitation and access, parent-time, dockets, bailiffs, statutes, decrees,* and *motions and affidavits in support of orders to show cause* as if they grew up on one of those television courtroom dramas. And let's not forget our Latin: *ex parte, pro se, im pro per, in limine, sua sponte, bifurcate, subpoena, duces tecum,* and *guardian ad litem.*

Your familiarity with this divorce vocabulary is usually in proportion to the level of your divorce conflict. To a couple separating on relatively good terms, preparing a simple affidavit may take all afternoon, while those experiencing a highly contested divorce become able to draft their own pleadings, effect service, and otherwise represent themselves in court with all the skill of an experienced lawyer.

But not all the words in the divorce dictionary are negative. Over the past twenty years, we have seen a slow shift in the way divorce is viewed. A more restorative, rather than punitive, approach has been applied to divorce in the courts. In fact, many states require alternative attempts to resolve the divorce before the court will intervene. With this shift in perception comes a new vocabulary with words such as *co-parent, interest-based negotiations, mediation, disclosure, win/win, parenting plan, understanding, proactive, truth of your experience, active listening, talking "circles," dialogue, healing,* and *peace.*

Finding Your "Source"

Imagine a high mountain spring feeding a stream that branches out as it flows down and covers the mountainside, giving life to the fields and valleys. We all have within us our own spring, or source, of energy that permeates our bodies, giving energy to our limbs and keeping us well and healthy. It is from this source that we derive our strength and remain healthy—emotionally, physically, and spiritually. And it is by drawing on a similar source that you can proceed with integrity and remain healthy through your divorce.

Integrity

It is important that we spend a moment discussing what we mean by *integrity*. Integrity is following through with what you say. It is the equalization of thought, word, and action. If you say it, you will do it. There is no need for the words, "I promise," or "I mean it," because when you act and live with integrity, people just know you will. Integrity can be a guide and a light to you in your sometimes dark world. You can draw strength from integrity. Its power is almost unmatched in today's society. There is no guile with integrity; there is no malice or ill feelings. Just as the needle of a compass always points to true north, living with integrity will prevent you from getting lost or being at the whim and mercy of feelings that have little real value.

Living with integrity means deciding what is important in your life and never deviating from that path. It means taking a journey to discover who you are, your bigger purpose, and your "true north," where you can always plant your feet and never turn from it. Living with integrity means controlling your thoughts, your words, your actions, and aligning them with that higher purpose you have set for yourself. From this source there is unlimited power from which you may draw.

Finding this center and source of power in your life will be the sure foundation upon which you build for the rest of your new relationship with your former spouse as you effectively raise and co-parent your children. If your center is strong and unwavering, your life will most likely be filled with peace and harmony. This does not mean that everything will always go your way, but it does mean that you can remain strong throughout, and have the skills and guidance to act in a productive and meaningful way. This centering is so important, that the next section is dedicated entirely to its concept and application.

Just Do It

Take a minute and reflect upon your life, this "new you."

1.   Is every hour of every day committed to some "cause"—worthy or not?
2.   What about your children's lives? Do they still have time to be a kid?
3.   What regular activities do you do to help you relax and "find yourself" amid the chaos and confusion that has entered your life?
4.   When was the last time you were "caught off guard" by something your former spouse said or did? How did you react? What was the result?
5.   What is the "center of gravity" in your life? Is it your faith? Is it something else?

SECTION II

CENTERING AND BALANCE

I have set the Lord always before me: because he is at my right hand, I shall not be moved.

—Psalms 16:8

But my disciples shall stand in holy places, and shall not be moved.

—Doctrine and Covenants 45:32

3

Finding Your Center

Centering is the art and process of achieving balance. Not just physically, but mentally, emotionally, and spiritually as well. We include all four elements of our life because all four are inseparably connected. Each affects the others in very real and profound ways. Strengthen one and you strengthen the others. Think back to the last time you had a really good workout, or played a challenging game of some sport. Do you remember how happy you felt afterwards, how much clearer your thoughts became, and how much more at peace you were with life? Recall the last time you had a brilliant thought or solved a mystery that you had been working on for a while. Was there a surge of energy that accompanied it? That was the physical fruit of a mental labor.

Centering is the focusing on the "within" instead of the "without." It is the first and ever-continuing step toward peace in your life and harmony with your surroundings. Centering is all about you—your strengths, your weaknesses, your perceptions, and your lenses from which you view and interpret the world around you. Being centered enables you to stand firm, and not be moved by the storm that rages around you. It is a strength that no one can take away from you. It is personal. It is spiritual. If you are not centered in life, you are like a ship, tossed to and fro.

What is Your Center?

Finding your center is a personal process. As we have mentioned already, your center must be something that comes from within. It must be something that no one—not your former spouse, not his attorney, not the judge, not anyone—can manipulate or take away. Many find their center in their faith. Perhaps it is your relationship with God, the quiet assurance that you are loved and that your prayers are not falling on deaf ears. But becoming centered is much more than simply believing. Your center becomes the source of your strength, the foundation to which you can anchor the many facets of your life to when you are faced with "shafts in the whirlwind."

A Sure Foundation

In the previous chapter we talked briefly about finding your "source" and related it to a mountain stream, watering and giving life to fields and valleys along its journey. As true as this might be, let's be real for a moment. Despite our (and other's) peaceful analogies, divorce is more often a raging storm, flooding your life with pain, woes, and doubts to the point that you may not catch your breath or keep your head above its murky waters. Your life may resemble the words of Helaman, from the Book of Mormon, full of mighty winds, and hail beating down upon you (Helaman 5:12).

Part of being centered in your new, post-divorce life is building on a strong foundation. Let's look at Helaman's words more closely and then apply them.

> And now, my sons, remember, remember that it is upon the rock of our Redeemer, who is Christ, the Son of God, that ye must build your foundation; that when the devil shall send forth his mighty winds, yea, his shafts in the whirlwind, yea, when all his hail and his mighty storm shall beat upon you, it shall have no power over you to drag you down to the gulf of misery and endless wo, because of the rock upon which ye are build, which is a sure foundation, a foundation whereon if men build they cannot fail.

Notice that we are not promised exception from the storm. Helaman does not say "if" the storm comes, but "when." We are not promised that the rain won't fall, or that we won't get wet, or that the storms and whirlwinds will pass us by. When these things happen, when he who would have us be miserable and damned as he is tries to suffocate us with fear and uncertainty, the promise is that we will not fall, that the raging storms will not have the power to drag us down to the pits of hell and despair. Will you get wet? Yes. Will you get bruised? Most likely. Will you survive with your faith intact and with a promise of a brighter tomorrow? Most assuredly.

Far too often good men and women lose their testimonies in the conflict that appears to engulf them, and they are washed away when the rain falls; they are knocked off balance when the storms of divorce blow in. *Do not move from that rock.* That foundation that can and will enable you to withstand every blow a divorce can deliver. Often people in the Church—bishops, neighbors, home and visiting teachers—do not understand what you are going through, cannot fathom the depth of pain and anguish you are suffering. But there is one who does, one who suffered the greatest grief and agony, who descended to the lowest pits of hell in order to succor his people—to comfort and help you. He understands, and he will never forsake you.

A Strong Center

Whether you are in the early stages of separation or a "frequent flyer" of the court, you must find (or create) and continually strengthen your own center point for your new life. This center point must be steady and independent of anyone or anything else. From this seed will grow the roots that ground you and keep you strong amid the storms that may rage around you. Your center need not be limited to a spiritual awakening. For some it is the love of their children or an unconditional acceptance of who they are and that they are doing the best they can. Some have developed personal mission statements to express their values, ethics, dreams, and goals, while others build their new life upon a religious or scriptural foundation. Still others find their own way and tap into their own sources of strength.

But whatever you choose as your center point and source of energy, it must be a focus on the "within" and something that you are capable of sustaining on your own, regardless of the actions or behaviors of others, especially your former spouse. So much of this book is dependent on becoming centered. From this center comes your strength and ability to apply these principles and practices to your own situation and conflict.

Managing Conflict from Your Center

A strong center will enable you to stand and not be moved by what happens around you. At the same time your center will allow you to be flexible and relaxed in your new life. The test of your centered state is not when things are going well, but when you are faced with challenges and problems. It is this firm flexibility that allows you to maintain your balance and, hence, your strength in the situation.

One of Aesop's fables, "The Reed and the Oak Tree," illustrates this principle very well. The story goes that during a storm, a large oak tree was uprooted by the wind and thrown across a stream. It fell among some reeds, which it thus addressed: "I wonder how you, who are so light and weak, are not entirely crushed by these strong winds." To this the reeds reply, "You fight and contend with the wind, and consequently you are destroyed; while we on the contrary bend before the least breath of air, and therefore remain unbroken, and escape."

The ability to move with an opposing force or attack can only be found when one is centered. In the above story, the reeds would not have been able to bend if they were not rooted and grounded to the earth. On a physical level, this story is true in your own life, maybe without you even knowing it. How, you might say, do I bend like a reed? Consider the last time you walked outside and were hit by a strong wind. Your first instinct is to pivot, turn your back to the wind, catch your balance, and protect your face and eyes from any sand, rain, or snow. You may still need to brave your way into the attacking wind, but first you turned with its force to give you time to evaluate your position, resources, and needs before acting. It is not hard to see how you can apply this principle to the practice of blending with the conflict you have with your former spouse.

> The key to good technique is to keep your hands, feet, and hips straight and centered. If you are centered, you can move freely. The physical center is your belly; if your mind is set there as well, you are assured of victory in any endeavor.
>
> –Morihei Ueshiba

Circle of Strength

It is common knowledge in the world of martial arts that physical strength is limited and confined to a small circle with the individual at the center. The further someone moves from that center, the more vulnerable he becomes. Strength cannot go beyond that circle. No matter how strong a man is, once he is extended beyond his circle, the ability to use that strength diminishes. Consider this simple exercise to illustrate this teaching. Stand up with your feet about shoulder width apart, knees slightly bent, if you wish. Feel how solid you are right now. You are balanced and secure in your stance. It would take considerable strength to move you or knock you down. Now reach out, keeping your feet planted, and stretch out as far as you can. Lean way out there. Stretched out like this, far from your center, the smallest child or slightest breeze could bring you down.

This principle applies to divorce and your new relationship with your former spouse. Just as your physical strength is diminished the further, you are stretched from your center, your emotional strength and control over your own lives diminishes the further you reach out from your own circle of strength and into someone else's. If you reach into that person's circle of strength, he will be strong and balanced every time. On the other hand, if someone reaches into yours . . .

Centering in Divorce Conflict

The court (or other conflict resolution professionals) sometimes label many families who experience chronic, high conflict "fragile." For these families it seems like the slightest problem or deviation from the way things "should" be knocks them "off balance" and throws their lives into a tailspin. When they are not centered, divorced parents react to the behaviors and imagined motives of the other with quick and extreme actions of their own. You can see, or possibly even know yourself, how this type of conflict escalates until nothing short of an act of God will bring the issues and concerns back into focus. Once off balance, it is difficult to regain your footing and find your center again. It can be done, however, and it must be done before a working relationship can begin to emerge and take shape.

Shed Expectations

This circle of strength philosophy and training has direct application to you and your divorce. When you divorce, any control you may have had over the other parent is gone. Many divorcing parents can leave their spouse but are unable to leave their spouse alone. Time, energy, mounting frustration, attorney's fees, and court costs are expended, and usually wasted, by one or both sides trying to control the other's behaviors, actions, words, and even thoughts. These parents find it hard to "disengage" from each other. They spend their time extending beyond their own circle of strength and reaching into their former spouse's life, looping and twisting this ever-increasing knot that keeps the two of them together. You cannot expect to divorce your spouse *and* control them at the same time. It cannot be done, but that does not stop many from trying.

> **The truth is we can't count on anything except our ability to choose how to respond to what happens to us.**
>
> –M. J. Ryan,
> *Attitudes of Gratitude*

One important key you must understand in order to move forward, find your center, and experience real peace is that some things in life are beyond your ability to control. Through no fault of your own, they are simply beyond your circle of strength. But beyond this realization, your thoughts and actions must reflect this understanding as well. This means forever discarding the "but" between what you know you should do or are expected to do and what you are going to do anyway ("I know he should see the children, but he must learn he can't treat me like that"). This means you must shed all expectations of controlling anything the other parent says or does.

Control

A word about control before we move on. Control is all about change. Think about it. If you could control someone's mind and make him do whatever you wanted him to do, the result is a change in his behavior. Similarly, threats or bribes are attempts to change someone's behavior. A parent extends care and exerts control over children to help them grow into adulthood. In the business world, if you have 51 percent of the control of a company, you have the ability to change the company to resemble your vision of the ideal business. When you are the one in control, you are the one to change the outcome.

But there is only one person we are in control of, and that is ourselves. Sure, you may be the "boss" at work, and have the power and leverage to control the work production of your employees, but take away the incentive of pay or the threat of being fired, and your "control" vanishes in an instant before your eyes. People do things for one of these two reasons: because they want to, or because they are afraid of the consequences of not doing it. It is just that simple. Your employer may have bought your back from nine to five, but not necessarily your heart. Threats or incentives may influence the choices you make day to day (such as go to work or get fired), but the control is still yours. So, if you can control *only* yourself, then you are the *only* one capable of changing yourself. The same goes for the other parent.

Two Lists

When we realize and accept that we cannot change someone else outright, something interesting happens. When you begin to realize and name the things in life that you can't control, you become aware of the things in your life that you can change. By making one list, you actually make two. It is a universal truth that there is opposition in all things—male and female, heaven and earth, yin and yang, up and down, forward and backward, life and death. There are things you can control in life, and there are things you can't. This is especially true in your relationship with your former spouse. As an exercise, let's make a list like the one we have been talking about.

Before we get started, though, we need to be clear that we are making *two* lists. Many people are quick to list the pages of faults or behaviors the other parent has and can't do anything about, but they draw a blank when it comes to what they can do. We'll get you started.

I Can't Control	I Can Control
• What the other parent thinks or says about me	• My thoughts and words about the other parent
• The other parent's religion or values	• My own morals and values
• The other parent's parenting skills	• Improving my own parenting skills

- The other parent's new romantic relationship

- The other parent's new lifestyle

- The other parent's household rules

- The other parent's reliability or punctuality

- The other parent's family members and their actions

- The judge's decision

- The statues and laws

- My choice in friends and partners

- My own healthy lifestyle

- My own consistent household rules

- Doing what I say I will do and always being there

- My conversations and instructions to my own family members

- My own compliance and attitude

- My willingness to accept and follow them

If you focus only on the list of things you can't control, there is a tendency to believe that the other parent's influence is somehow stronger than you own. You become a victim to the other parent's "wrongs," and your frustration grows over your inability to control or change them. The "harm" they are committing somehow overshadows the "good" that you have worked so hard to achieve. This occurs most often when there is a disagreement or conflict over morals or religion. Though you must always be on your guard, for example, it is foolish to believe that the other parent's lack of morals is going to automatically negate all of your hard work to teach your children right from wrong.

What You Can Control

Why is this the case? What makes the other parent's influence so strong and yours so weak? Nothing. It only appears this way when you are off balance. But many of you will say, "What if the values *are* incompatible and on extreme ends of the spectrum? Doesn't this confuse children to be taught one thing in one home only to be taught something different in the other?" It might surprise you that the answer is yes. It does confuse the child, but a child's life is full of such confusion. Children may learn one value at home or in church, and then see its opposite glorified on television or at the movies. Lessons and values taught in the home are ridiculed and undermined at school. What are we to do?

Lock our children up in their rooms and give them no contact with the outside world? Of course not. These tests try their faith and upbringing and shape them into strong and responsible adults.

Again, you can do little to control someone else. You can no more stop the sun from setting in the west or the rain from falling than you can control and change the other parent. If you try, you will be met with incredible resistance and even personal attacks. But just as the sun sets despite your attempts to stop it, you are not forced to remain in the dark. Remember your two lists? You could build a fire, turn on a light, light a candle, or you may take in the beauty of the stars that were hidden by the sunlight. The rain may fall, but you need not get wet. You could seek shelter, or use an umbrella, or do something else . . . you get the picture. As this is important to becoming and remaining centered, we will say it again: there are some things in life that you have no control over.

Hidden Strength

Does this make you weak? *No!* In fact, it is just the opposite. Knowing what you can't control frees up energy and resources to affect the things you can. It gives you strength. It gives you a choice. You cease being a *reactive* person, and instead, become a *proactive* one. A proactive person has choice; a reactive one doesn't. You may not have control over the other parent's words and actions, but you do not have to be at his mercy. You will always have the capacity to choose your response to whatever the other parent may do. You become *response*-able. The other parent may reach into your circle of strength, and you may have to respond accordingly, but if you are centered, it is the other parent who is off balance, and you who remain sure and steady. Staying rooted in your own center point enables you to remain balanced. No more "flying off the handle," or warning that "you give me no other choice." This new control over your own life will enable you to change, and this change will be noticed. Your relationship with the other parent will begin to change. With new balance, and armed with this "response"-ability, you will begin to see order emerge from chaos. Your life will take on a new shape. Like clay centered on a potter's wheel, you will finally be able to mold and shape your new life.

A Subtle Destroyer

Being centered and balanced means resisting being acted upon by outside forces beyond your circle of strength. You know who you are and what is important to you. Being centered also means you are not reaching beyond your own circle of strength in futile attempts to control or change someone else. When you are centered and balanced, no one can control you. It is that simple. It is not that easy, but it *is* that simple.

In almost every divorce, though, a malicious fiend lurks, waiting to undermine and sabotage your efforts to resolve the issues, move on, and find the peace you deserve. A cruel word, an action that hurt or offended you, a lie, a cheat, or a violation of trust or intimacy can bore a hole in your heart and refuse to leave. Even though the events may have long since passed, the feelings you have toward the other parent continue to affect you in the most unpleasant ways, exerting control over you, and keeping the pain you felt alive. Thus, an important step toward becoming centered and balanced is forgiveness.

Forgiveness

Now, when we talk of forgiveness here, we do not mean the kind of forgiveness that involves confession to free ourselves from the burden of sin. Nor is it the "forgive and forget" that is all too easy to talk about but, unless you have memory lapses, impossible to do. Forgiveness, as discussed here, is a letting go, a freedom attained by refusing to be manipulated and affected by an outside force that you have little or no control over. Forgiveness is also about moving forward with life.

A Healing Journey

To move forward with purpose and direction, you must first know where you are. To quote Lao Tzu, the great Chinese philosopher and author of the *Tao Te Ching*, "The journey of a thousand leagues starts from where your feet stand."[1] Notice here that this great journey does *not* begin with the first step, as we have all heard, but from where you stand. Unless you are just floating through life, drifting aimlessly from minute to minute, day to day, year in and year out, you must know where you *are* before you can begin to chart out a map and *go* anywhere. This is true in every aspect of life.

If you go to a financial advisor with the expectation that he will help you reach your goal of becoming a millionaire, you will spend a good deal of time painting a detailed and accurate financial picture of where you stand today. Only then can you make plans for the first and thousandth step toward your goal. If you are lost and call a friend for directions, the first question he will ask is, "Where are you?" If you can't answer him by at least giving him landmarks or street intersections, he can do nothing for you, and you will remain lost.

Similarly, if you want to create a better, more peaceful relationship with your former spouse, you first need to know the place and condition of where you stand today. So, to paraphrase Lao Tzu, where do you stand?

When we are betrayed, or when someone strikes at our heart, our reputation, our friendships, or our loved ones, we lose something—trust, relationship, dreams, or our good name. With that loss comes pain—not just the mental or emotional pain that puts a damper on our day, but in many circumstances, the pain that causes real physical ailments. Our hearts and our minds don't just feel burdened or hurt, we can also get nauseous, break out in hives, or develop or aggravate existing medical conditions. And we don't just feel this way once (when the offense happened), but every time we visit the spot where it happened, see our offender, or think about what happened. Again, we can see the link between the spiritual, mental, and physical—the connection between the "within" and the "without." Perhaps it is here, amid your internal and external pain, that you stand at the beginning of your journey.

People will tell you to just get over it, get up and on your own two feet again. They are minimizing what you are dealing with through the well-intentioned guise of offering help. But don't fool yourself. The pain and feelings of loss experienced by families—especially children—of divorce is said to be greater than the pain and loss felt after the death of a parent or spouse. Many counselors, therapists, and mediators believe that families of divorce suffer real trauma trying to adjust and pick up the pieces of their lives and dreams.

> **The weak cannot forgive. Forgiveness is an attribute of the strong.**
> —Gandhi

You must *not* ignore the pain and unpleasant feelings. Instead of sweeping them under the proverbial rug and pretending you're okay, you must confront and identify them. Only then is there hope of putting these painful events behind you and finally moving forward with your life. This process of identifying your feelings should include some level of counseling, whether with a psychologist, therapist, clergy, or mentor. This is not the same as going to a friend and unloading all your complaints and problems. Find a professional who is not afraid of, or uncomfortable with your pain and who can guide you safely through the storms raging inside of you.

Just as a doctor must diagnose the symptoms to identify the illness before he can prescribe a cure, you must acknowledge and embrace the pain and grief you are feeling before you can take that first step on your healing journey.

They say that time heals all. This is a lie. Time may be helpful to reflect on the event and your feelings, but time itself does not heal. If left unresolved and unattended to, pain turns into suffering, and offenses can grow and fester until they are beyond your ability to heal them on your own. Time gives you only one thing: time. What you do with that time will determine whether your pain passes away into peace.

Do It For You

So what does it take to forgive someone who has hurt you or done you wrong? When this question is asked, the answer that comes first to mind is simple: an apology. This would seem logical, but this simple answer is deceiving and is potentially damaging to a balanced and centered state. There is a shift of power and responsibility when you wait for an apology. When you require an apology from your offender before letting go of the pain, you give them power over you and the way you feel. If they never apologize, you'll never forgive them, and you'll keep hold of those negative feelings. Why would anyone do this? Sometimes the one who has caused so much pain doesn't even know they have done anything wrong. To wait for the words "I'm sorry" is to delay your healing and sense of peace.

When it comes right down to it, apology or not, we forgive someone when we *choose* to forgive them. Think of the times in your life when you continued to feel bad and carry a grudge even after the words "I'm sorry" have been uttered. This is because there is nothing magical about the words "I'm sorry" that repair and heals the wounds and makes amends in our life. It may soften your heart to see their remorse, making it *easier* for you to forgive, but there again, you *choose* when and where to forgive. When you are centered and balanced, you can choose to forgive and let go of offenses, and you are no longer under someone's control. Consider the words of Gordon B. Hinkley:

> How difficult it is for any of us to forgive those who have injured us. We are all prone to brood on the evil done us. That brooding becomes as a gnawing and destructive canker. . . . I submit that it takes neither strength nor intelligence to brood in anger over wrongs suffered, to go through life with a spirit of vindictiveness, to dissipate one's abilities in planning retribution. There is no peace in the nursing of a grudge. There is no happiness in living for the day when you can "get even."[2]

But does forgiveness mean you give your offender a clean slate and "forgive and forget," accepting or condoning what they have done, like it's all okay? Of course not. There is a common saying, "Fool me once, shame on you; fool me twice, shame on me." Forgiving someone who has violated your trust or hurt you in some way does not mean you have to pretend like it didn't happen or give him another opportunity to repeat his offenses. You may need to take steps to protect yourself from being the victim twice, redefine the relationship, and take certain precautions to see that you are not hurt again; however, let go of the feelings associated with the offense. Forgiveness is not for the offendor's benefit—it is for yours. You are the one in control; you are centered and at peace.

And so, with your feet planted firmly and completely within your circle of strength, equipped with a list of those things in your life that you *can* control, and having forgiven yourself as well as those who have trespassed against you, you are ready to take the next step and turn your attention to the other parent's needs.

Just Do It

Before we move on, however, take a few minutes and really think about what we have just covered here. Becoming centered is the key to a new, happy, and healthy life. If you are off balance during this time of your life, you will more likely experience the grief and pain so common in divorce.

1. What brings you comfort during this time of your life? Is this your center?
2. What else "defines" you?
3. Do you regularly spend time outside of your circle of strength?
4. Are you in the habit of making one list or two?
5. Have you really forgiven the events associated with the divorce? Can you think and speak about them without knots in your stomach?

NOTES

1. Lao Tzu, *Tao Teh Ching*, trans. by John C.H. Wu (Shambhala Publications, Inc., 1990).
2. Gordon B. Hinckley, "Of You It Is Required to Forgive," *Ensign*, June 1991, 20.

4

Win/Win: A Test of Balance

The principle of Win/Win is the principle of mutual benefit, so says Stephen Covey, author of the *Seven Habits of Highly Effective People* and one of the world's foremost experts on personal development and empowerment. This mutual benefit doesn't mean that everyone gets what they start out saying they want, but that, in the end, everyone possesses and walks away with what they need. Win/Win is safety. Win/Win is respect and balance. In other words, Win/Win means that no one gets hurt.

No One Gets Hurt

The world around us is filled with violence. Watch thirty seconds of the evening news, and you'll see the dark and desperate underside of civilization and glimpse momentarily into man's heart of darkness. Glamorized in movies and music, violence is settling in for an extended stay in our society. It seems we cannot escape it. Violence, like a disease, spreads and spawns more violence, often disguised in the name of humanity. "Peacekeeping" troops move through the rubble of war-ravaged cities atop tanks, keeping an ever-watchful eye on the populace, ready at a moment's command to open fire and keep the peace. Peace that must be maintained by force is not peace at all. Force does not beget peace. Force begets force.

> **Treat a man as he is and he will remain as he is. Treat a man as he can and should be and he will become as he can and should be.**
>
> —Goethe

We'll show you what we mean. Try this. Ask a friend to stand facing you and clench your hand into a fist and extend it toward your friend. Invite your friend to do the same. There, with knuckles squared off against knuckles, and without giving any instruction or explanation, gently start pushing toward your friend, gradually applying more and more pressure. Without saying a word, your friend will begin pushing back. It seems to come naturally. Force, as it seems, invites more force.

Divorce as a "Win/Win" Relationship

Society has been feeding us half-truths and lies since we were children on the elementary school playground with respect to conflict resolution. We were brought up to believe that you either win or you lose, you're either tough or you're soft, and if you're not strong, you must be weak. This either/or connection results in two regrettable courses of action—you can either teach the co-parent a lesson and fight back, *or* you let the co-parent get away with everything and give him an invitation to walk all over you again. If you don't put a stop to it now, you set yourself up for a lifetime of misery. In each case, at least one of you ends up getting hurt.

These same lies are perpetuated throughout your divorce—either you get custody of the children or your former spouse does; if you don't pull out the big guns and defend your rights before the judge, the other parent and her attorney will take you for everything you've got. And the scenarios just go on and on. But when everything is settled during your day in court (that took two years and twenty thousand dollars to get to), you are left to work out the rest of your lives *together*. If you have childre n in common, a co-parenting relationship is the end result of your divorce. Period. Whether you fought it and ended your dreams for happiness in a trial before a disgusted judge or parted ways peacefully at the outset, in the end, the two of you are required by law to share your children and work together to raise your children the best you can. Like it or not, your former spouse becomes your parenting partner, and unlike what you thought would happen, you are not free of that man or woman forever. On the contrary, the day you separate becomes the first day of your new relationship. Hurting your co-parent physically, mentally, emotionally, or financially will only serve to fuel the fire of retribution and justification.

"Win"ing Combinations

Where few of us have had good success with Win/Win over the course of our lives, perhaps it would be helpful to identify other "win"ing and losing combinations, and what they might look like in the world of divorce co-parenting.

Win/Lose. This combination is the most prevalent in our society. Win/ Lose is when you win or reach your goal, want, or need at the expense of someone else. Thoughts and justifications for these outcomes may include, "Finders keepers, losers weepers" (which is great unless you are the loser), "you snooze you lose," or "Hey, they deserve what they get." This Win/Lose philosophy is what controls and drives most sporting events and makes them fun to watch. No one would tune into the Super Bowl if the two teams combined their efforts to see how many goals they could score together. Sporting events, games, and regulated competitions fall into this category. By design, there must be a winner and a loser, and ne'er the twain shall meet. Even ties are settled in sudden death showdowns.

In a conflicted divorce, Win/Lose usually involves the hiring of bulldog attorneys, hell-bent on defending your legal rights, and punishing your former spouse for all the mean things she did you while you were married. You pull no punches in your push to win the house, the kids, the boat, the nicer car, the retirement, and everything else that should be yours. The problem is that your former spouse does the same. Battle lines are drawn, opposing goals declared, and you each move quickly to get the upper hand. It is all about winning, or at least making sure that you don't lose.

Lose/Win. This is the martyr's paradise. Sometimes used as a crutch, Lose/Win is simply giving in or giving up to avoid some future conflict. You let your former spouse walk all over you because you think it is wrong to fight back or because (truth be told) you lack the courage. You play the victim, unwilling to take a stand for your wants and needs. You meet everyone else's needs and back down at the first sign of conflict, setting the stage for a repeat in the future. You give and give and give, and feel miserable before, during, and after. You may try to kid yourself into thinking that there is some higher goal or purpose for your behavior, but you know there isn't. And although we should be careful to distinguish between one who loses and one who is selfless, those in a Lose/Win relationship know who they are, but they don't know how to do it any other way.

Lose/Lose. This is the most destructive kind of conflict resolution. In these "solutions," each side in the dispute would rather destroy or lose forever something of value than let the other side have it or enjoy it. This is the "If I can't have it, then no one can" attitude. Acts of vandalism are often Lose/Lose motivated. A criminal sees that your new car is equipped with an anti-theft device and suddenly their intentions shift from wanting to take the car to just seeing you don't enjoy it either. The criminal does this by damaging the car in any way he can.

Lose/Lose is abundant in the field of divorce. Nothing is more horrifying than to watch parents who have an unusually high-conflict divorce apply this Lose/Lose outcome to their co-parenting relationship. This might happen, for example, when one parent gets remarried and goes on a week-long honeymoon, "hiding" the children at grandma's house instead of letting them stay with the other parent. Or when one parent would rather keep the kids at home, "punishing" them with nothing to do but to watch old reruns on TV than let them go to a baseball game with their other parent because it is not his scheduled time or weekend. It doesn't take long before Lose/Lose actions escalate the conflict to a level where threats are made and drastic and dangerous measures taken by one or both parents. If disregard for their children's interests and needs is severe enough, parents can lose the right to see them and they may be placed with an extended family member or adopted out. Over time, Win/Lose and Lose/Win relationships eventually become Lose/Lose relationships. Unless you actively seek a Win/Win solution to your conflict, the painful experiences will become too much for you to bear.

A Time and a Place

On occasion, and used sparingly, each of these "win"ing combinations may be appropriate and beneficial to painting the larger resolution picture. You will recall the five general strategies for dealing with conflict: avoidance, accommodation, competition, compromise, and collaboration. Each of these strategies fit into one of the four "win"ing combination. For example, competition would be a Win/Lose scenario; accommodation would be Lose/Win; while both avoidance and compromise have the markings of Lose/Lose. Only through collaboration can you attain Win/Win.

As we said, there is a time and a place for each of these strategies and philosophies when it comes to resolving resolution. For example, there are plenty of times where accommodation (Lose/Win) would be the best strategy to apply to a conflict. You may see how important something is to the other parent and just give in. That's okay. Your actions may open the door to other acts of kindness in return. Lose/Win becomes destructive when you are the only one giving in and giving up. Sometimes the issue in conflict may not be that important to either one of you and the two of you compromise, each walking away with less than you wanted or needed, but enough to walk away peacefully. But for matters of great importance to one or both of you—say, the raising of your children and working toward meeting their needs—collaboration and Win/Win must be the internal compass you follow and the driving force behind your thoughts and deeds.

You know what a Win/Win resolution looks like, so how do you create one? Though simple, it is not easy. A Win/Win outcome in a divorced co-parenting relationship is a continuing process of seeing, understanding, and meeting both yours and the other parent's needs.

Positions and Interests

Remember the definition we used for conflict in Chapter One? Conflict is the interaction of interdependent people who have, or at least think they have, incompatible goals and perceive interference from each other. Put another way, conflict occurs when people have shared interests but have opposing positions and plans for meeting and satisfying them. Positions are *what* people say they want, while their interests are the reasons *why* they want it.

There is a great teaching scenario involving an orange that addresses some of the differences between positions and interests. Imagine that two people want an orange, but there is only one left. They both insist on having it, but neither is willing to give in. What is your first thought to resolve this dilemma? Cut it in half, right? Each gets half. After all it's only fair. It turns out, however, that one wanted the pulp for making juice, while the other wanted the rind to bake a cake. When you know and understand someone's underlying interests and needs (what they *really* want), many more options for resolution surface. We seldom take the time to explore someone else's reasons for wanting what they say they want. We accept it, reject it, or find some middle ground. We have been taught to compromise quickly to each other's positions without taking the time to discover the underlying interest driving those positions.

Positions could be explained as the means to achieving the end. They are usually fixed and specific. Positions are your own solutions to the problem without taking into account all of the facts or the other side of the story. Positions are the demands placed on another person, or the stipulations or conditions built into coming to an agreement or understanding. "It's her way or the highway" is a good description of a position; it's what she wants and that's all there is to it. In medium-to-high conflict situations, positions are extreme and used to bargain with. Bargaining, as you will remember, is a series of back and forth offers and counteroffers used to reach some acceptable middle ground. The stakes in bargaining usually begin much higher than what you expect to get, giving you room to play the game and negotiate down to a settlement that is closer to fair. Bargaining is the attorney who files a complaint seeking a million dollars in damages when he'd be happy with a hundred bucks, or the used car salesman who starts out asking a new car price for last year's model with thirty thousand miles on it.

Although this type of bargaining is acceptable, and even expected, on used car lots, positional bargaining is a poor strategy for resolving conflicts with your former spouse. Bargaining from your position is based on manipulation and deception, and usually skirts around the real issues. These real issues are at the center of the conflict and may, in fact, have very little to do with what you thought you were arguing about.

Interests, then, are a bit more difficult to uncover. While most people are not shy about telling you what they want, they rarely explain the underlying reasons for wanting it. Some might not even know what those reasons are. They are usually buried pretty deep, especially if the conflict is high and the trust of others is low. But do not fear. In fact, you know many of these interests, whether you realize it or not.

We all share common interests and needs. For example, we all share the need for food and water, shelter and safety, and a sense of purpose. Similarly, people going through a divorce have needs in common too. They are likely to include a place to live, means to support themselves and their children, freedom to move on and live their own life, to love, and be loved. If you possess any of these needs, you can bet that your and co-parent has them too. It may be unsettling to admit that you are more alike than you are different, but being centered and balanced in your own life gives you permission to accept this fact.

When these needs are threatened, people sometimes take desperate actions to protect them. Parents have been known to kidnap their own children when threatened that the former spouse will never let them see their children again. They take the children and run, hiding under assumed names, while the other parent hires private investigators to track them down. Cruel or threatening words are spoken, extreme positions are taken, and Win/Lose or Lose/Win scenarios quickly turn into Lose/Lose. When it is over, incredible damage has been done, lines have been crossed that cannot be easily crossed back, the conflict escalates, and parents and children are left to suffer in the wake of consequences.

Unfortunately, a Win/Win resolution is not as easy as meeting these few and basic needs. It is a start, to be sure, but your new co-parenting relationship is going to be filled with conflicts and problems unique to you and your circumstances. There are maturity levels to consider, different values and ethics, and the ever-present influence of family and friends. If you are going to succeed in resolving these conflicts in a way where no one gets hurt, you must look beyond her stated positions, what she wants or does, discover her underlying interests and needs, and help meet them. But how can you do this? Stop your talking, put your own needs and agenda aside, pause a moment, and *listen*.

Just Do It

The concept of Win/Win is easy for people to talk about but is difficult to accept and practice. Win/Win is equivalent to the Golden Rule: treating others as you would want to be treated yourself. This is hard to do when someone you once loved has hurt you. His acts and their painful consequences may cause you to feel that he doesn't deserve this higher treatment—let him feel what it's like to lose for once. But it is a straightforward fact that anything other than a Win/Win resolution to conflict will result in more pain and suffering for everyone, including your children.

1. Are you centered enough to consider your former spouse's wants and needs?
2. List at least five instances when you have reached a Win/Win resolution to problems with your former spouse.
3. Can you think of instances when you have reached Win/Lose outcomes with your former spouse?
4. Can you think of instances when you have reached Lose/Lose solutions?
5. If you are having troubles right now, do you know what it is you want? Can you articulate why you want it?
6. What are some of the needs your former spouse has? Can you think of ways to help him or her achieve them?

If you aren't centered enough to consider your former spouse's needs, don't worry. It will take time. It will take a sincere effort to undo many of those harmful and negative thoughts and feelings you may still be harboring. Change doesn't happen overnight.

SECTION III

RELATIONSHIP

Understanding is a wellspring of life unto him that hath it.

—Proverbs 16:22

5

The Art of Listening

Up to this point, we have focused primarily on what you can do, independent of your former spouse, to prepare yourself for the change divorce brings. It is no accident that so much about influencing your views about conflict, divorce as a whole, and what you can do to survive—and even thrive—during this time of your life has taken up nearly half of this book. Only when

> **The beginning of wisdom is to call things by their right names.**
> —Chinese proverb

you are centered and can see the forest for the trees, so to speak are you in a position to make real change in your life and the lives of those around you.

Now, however, begins the interactive instruction. It's time to roll up your sleeves, take a deep breath, and move beyond the hypothetical and internal training, and jump right into practical and realistic ways to handle and resolve conflict when it arises between you and your former spouse. And the first step to resolving any problem is to identify and understand it. How can you do this? It's simple: listen.

Listening

Just as the journey of a thousand leagues begins from where you stand, you must know what the problems is—the *real* problem—before you can take

> **To understand a man's mind, listen to his words**
> –from a Chinese fortune cookie

steps toward resolving it. You must get behind it, examine it, and understand its true shape and form before an effective resolution can be created. If you have any hope of resolving the problems and disagreements that you have with your former spouse, you must get behind his position and understand his concerns and interests. Only then will you create a Win/Win solution and introduce peace into your own life, your co-parent's life, and the lives of your children.

Listening is the key. It is the single most important skill to having positive and productive communication. It doesn't matter how well you articulate your point or how much you present to prove your case, if the hearer doesn't really hear or understand you, then you would be better talking to a brick wall. "But," you ask, "how can I make my former spouse listen to me?" You can't. But you can make it *easier* for them to listen to you by first listening to them.

Listening does not come naturally. We live in a world that is all about us. It is a "me" generation. We are bombarded from every angle with marketing slogans and media tags telling us that we deserve the best, that second place just isn't good enough. We are so afraid of losing that all our time and energy is spent making sure our own point of view comes out on top and that we win. *You* need to be heard, *your* needs and wants are paramount in life, *and you* are somehow *entitled* to have it all. The result of this misinformation is that everyone seems to be talking, but no one is listening.

What Listening Isn't

For most of us, listening usually means that we are not the one doing the talking. But even though our mouths aren't running, our minds are. During an argument, we tend to use the time we have while the other person is speaking to prepare and organize what we are going to say next. We are getting ready to strike back and little listening takes place. Because our intent is to prove our point and convince the other side that we are right—and, consequently, that

> **Diplomacy is the art of saying "nice doggy" until you can find a rock.**
> —Will Rogers

he or she is wrong—we tend to ignore what the other is saying. Why would we take the time to listen to something that you know for a *fact* is wrong?

If we do listen at all, we only hear what we want to hear—literally. We engage in what is called "selective listening." We listen for key words or phrases that we can argue against and prove are incorrect or points that the other person might raise that could weaken our own position. When we do this, we cannot hear anything else. It is an auditory phenomenon. A well-known exercise and game illustrates this quite well. In this exercise, a small group of people stands shoulder-to-shoulder forming a small circle. Each holds a small button or piece of candy, while another reads a short story about the Wright family's vacation. Whenever the group hears the word "(W)right" they pass their object to the person on their right, and when they hear the word "left," they pass it to their left. The story then follows the Wright family leaving, taking rights at corners and wondering if they left the iron on, and otherwise having a right, good old time. It is all the participants can do to keep up with all of the lefts and rights. When the story is done, the reader asks them what the story was about and what happened. No one can repsonsd with any certainty. One or two may remember an incident here and there, but no one was listening to the story; the participants were only listening for certain words. This is what usually happens when we argue or have a disagreement. We listen for others to slip up, contradict themselves, or say things that support our argument, and miss the rest of the story and what they are trying to say.

Sometimes our not listening spills over into talking over each other. This is the least effective means of communication. It has been shown that it is physically impossible to talk and listen at the same time. If your mental energies are focused on talking and proving your point, your ability to listen and understand shuts off.

What Listening Is

When we speak of *really* listening, we don't only mean hearing the words that are spoken, but also hearing the words that are not. It goes beyond taking the words at face value to listening with your heart, as well. The Chinese character for the verb "to listen" is made up of five smaller characters: you, eyes, heart, ears, and undivided attention. There can be no better definition.

Communication is better and more meaningful when those in dispute are in the same room and can see each other. For this reason mediation sessions are conducted with the disputants sitting at the same table whenever possible. So much of our communication is non-verbal. There are some studies that claim that up to 90 percent of our communication is non-verbal. What we are trying to say, or how we really feel, is carried in the way we sit, what we do while we're listening, the amount of eye-to-eye contact we have, or the expressions on our face.

Is our heart in it? Do we care about what the other person is saying? Do we care about his problems? Can we empathize, or at least sympathize, with him? Can we believe him without abandoning our issues and concerns, acknowledging a difference of opinion or experience without trampling it underfoot? Do we listen to every word and take the time to make sure we really know what he is trying to say? Are we distracted? Have we lost interest in what he is telling us (what he says is wrong, after all), letting our thoughts drift to our own response and retaliation, or worse, what's on the television later that evening? Are we present with him?

The purpose of listening is to understand. If you are in a disagreement with someone, you may have heard every word she said, and even be able to repeat the words back, but still not understand what she is saying or why she is saying it. You haven't really listened. True listening involves more than just a keeping your mouth shut, although that's part of it. It is more than simply nodding in all the right places, and adding the occasional "uh-huh" and "hmm" when a pause permits. It is not just pretending to hear what the other person is saying and giving all the signs for *her* benefit—it is a willingness to leave your own position for a while, take off your shoes, and try hers on for size. Listening means working to understand, and the only way to do that is to take the excellent Native American advice buried deep within the cliché: walk a mile in the other person's moccasins.

> **The deepest hunger of the human heart is to be understood.**
> —Stephen R. Covey

Shoulder-to-Shoulder

To do this you must be able to "see" the problem as the other person sees it. You must stand shoulder-to-shoulder with him and join in his experience and his interpretation of the truth. Standing next to him, you begin to see things as he sees them. This is scary for most of us. Perhaps for the first time, you will move *next to* your opponent instead of either confronting him head on or turning your back and walking away. This can be quite unsettling. Questions start creeping into your mind—"What if he's right? What if it *does* look like I'm the bad guy here? Does it make me one?" Resist the urge to shut down, fight back, or get defensive against what you hear, and honestly see what the world looks like from where he's standing and through his eyes. Just stand in his shoes for a minute. Get the feel of them before you take that first step.

So you listen. Your intentions are honorable as you venture into unknown territory with only some vague advice you read somewhere to guide you. But what you hear couldn't be further from the truth. You listen as some event is described, but that's not the way it happened at all. You should know. You were there, after all. You didn't say those things. In fact, it was she who . . . But you suddenly stop yourself and remember that you're not on trial here, and return your focus to what your former spouse is saying.

Your first reaction may be to get upset, stop her dead in her tracks, and call her a liar. How could she say such things? You sense that she might actually believe what she's saying, but how can she? You were there and the event as she describes just didn't play out that way. She believes that she's right, but you're certain that you are. You both can't be right, can you?

If you are centered and balanced, you don't have to move very far to neutralize an attack. In fact, you don't really move anywhere at all. Instead you pivot and spin from your center, keeping firmly grounded within your own circle of strength and power. This pivoting is the key to listening and understanding. Moving from your center, you are free to face any direction you wish without moving anywhere or being knocked off balance. You don't have to agree with her, nor does her perception of events and of you make it true for you, but you can now admit and understand that it is true for her.

Oh Say, What Is Truth?

What we are about to say may fly in the face of everything you may have been taught and shake the foundation of what you think you know, especially as it affects the world of conflict resolution: there is no truth, only experience; there is no reality, only perception. Let us explain.

Thousand of dollars are spent in attorney's fees arguing and proving the truth in court, and in the end, it is up to a judge to decide what really happened and who did, or didn't, do what. This is frustrating to the judge, the attorneys, and the parties standing before the bench awaiting a decision. A casual observer might think that it is obvious someone is lying. But in fact, it's not that obvious—or simple—at all.

The Truth of Your Experience

You *both* may be right. But that's impossible, isn't it? You say she was late for the exchange, she says you were. She says you threatened her, when you clearly remember that she was hostile during the confrontation. This disagreement over the facts is common to most, if not all, disputes, and it is why we say that there is no truth, only experience.

An example is used in mediation training to explain that there may be more than one truth for any given situation. It is called "The Truth of Your Experience," and the scenario goes like this. Two people are in a room together. One says that the room is hot and—*look!*—he's got sweat on his brow to prove it. The other says it is cold and—*look!*—he's got goose bumps to prove it. Which one is right? Is the room hot or cold? And it's not just a matter of opinion to them; they each have proof to support their claim. Taking the example a little bit further, would it help to set up a thermometer to discover the exact temperature of the room, and then argue that the other person can't possibly be hot or cold given the fact of the temperature reading? No. This will not change their experience, their *truth* of being either hot or cold.

Truth Hurts

One tough question you must ask yourself is if there is any validity to the other person's experience. Justified or not, have your actions caused or contributed to the negative experience? Put in another way, you have to ask yourself if you are at least partially at fault here. If so, an apology would be in order. If you are justified, your apology might not be for the action itself, but for the effect it had on them, and then offer a commitment to work something out or handle things differently from here on out.

This goes to the heart of taking *blame* for something versus taking *responsibility* for your part in it. It's "not my fault" vs. "I played at least some part" in the conflict. You may have had good reasons to withhold the children and stop them from going with their other parent last weekend, but you cannot deny the part you played in stopping the parenting time. Just being aware of this can go a long way to understanding the other parent and her frustrations. You are taking those first few steps in her moccasins.

Question Your Assumptions

It is important to let the other parent tell his own story. It is equally important that you accept the experience as his truth. This is impossible, though, if you already know the reasons why he is doing what he is doing. You may *know* that he is interfering with your parent-time because he is still angry over the divorce and is using the kids as pawns to get at and hurt you. But do you really *know* this? It may look this way, and this may be your experience, but it does not make it "the truth." To listen and understand the other parent, you must disregard, or at least question, your assumptions about the other parent's behavior or actions.

Custody and parent-time disputes can be some of the most challenging and emotionally charged issues to mediate and resolve. In almost every case, each parent has come up with an explanation for the problems he or she has and "knows" that the other parent only cares about the money (child support), or is poisoning the children's minds so they won't like him or her, or is still angry about the divorce, and the list goes on and on. But what if the other parent doesn't just hate you? What if she isn't using the children as pawns, despite what it looks like? What if there is more to it?

Someone cuts you off on the freeway, and you may be tempted to curse and offer a blunt, one-finger critique of his driving skills. What you don't see is the little child in the backseat cut and bleeding as her father rushes her to the hospital. Let's say you show up on Friday night to pick up your children for the weekend, and the house is dark and no one is home. You might be swept up in a flood of negative emotion as you tell yourself the "reasons" she doesn't have the children there and ready. But before you surrender to your first and most damaging explanation of why the house is empty, pause and entertain the possibility, however remote, that you might not know why they weren't home.

Ask yourself why a rational and good parent would do this. (And your answer cannot be that the other parent isn't).

We all do things from time to time that others might question. However crazy our actions seem to others, we do them because they make perfect sense to us. A motorcycle daredevil prepares to jump an abysmal precipice, or a street magician encases himself in a block of ice and then is buried six feet underground. Crazy, right? But their actions make perfect sense to them. On an extreme end, even criminals can justify their crimes. It doesn't make what they did right, but it may shed some light on and better explain their behavior.

Summary

Listening may just be the most important element of good and effective communication. You can practice your arguments in front of a mirror until you believe you could pass the state bar exam with your presence and delivery, but if the other side does not feel like it has been heard, you can be sure that the other side is not going to listen to a word you say. But listening to understand is much harder than most of us think. Truly listening means that we not simply "stop talking," but that we set aside our own arguments and view, and try to see things as the other parent does. Right or wrong—it doesn't really matter. If the other parent believes it, then it is true for him or her (even if it's not true for you). The sooner you can accept this the sooner you will be able to diffuse the most volatile part of any disagreement and start working toward a peaceable solution.

Just Do It

Listening takes a strong will and a sure foundation (being centered, remember?) to stand there, unmoved, as you listen to what your former spouse has to say. Her truth may not match up with your truth, and you may be tempted to throw your hands up in the air and call it quits. Before you do, however, consider the following questions:

1. Are you listening to understand, or are you just going through the motions? Do you really want to know her answers?
2. Can you see, or at least accept the possibility, that her experience is "true" for her?
3. Do you *know* why your former spouse did what she did even before she answers? Can you question your assumptions?
4. With a friend (if possible), practice listening to an opposing point of view, setting aside your own beliefs and ideas as you try to see from another perspective. Was it easy? What was hard about it?

6

Frequently Asked Questions

Let's take a break and see where we are. So far you've agreed to listen first and are committed to trying to understand the other parent's concerns and complaints. Aided by the knowledge that each of you may have had different experiences so far, and thereby have different truths, you sit there, in person (preferably) or on the phone, with open ears, eyes, and hearts. What you hear, though, is unbelievable. Remember, though, that most people engaged in conflict begin by expressing their positions, their definition of the problem, and their well thought-out, but one-sided, solution. Positions, as you will recall, are usually framed in black or white, right or wrong, take it or leave it offers. Very little mediation and Win/Win negotiation can take place when you are working with positions. The best you can do is compromise and hope to cut your losses. So how do you find out what the other parent's "underlying" interests are? Ask.

Questions

A mediation practice is built on questions. Effective mediators constantly remind themselves that they have nothing to say to the parents—only questions to ask them. You would be wise to remember this as you forge or strengthen your co-parenting relationship. And just like everything else in conflict resolution, there are good questions and there are bad questions. Some are constructive and helpful in uncovering the underlying concerns and interests, while others are manipulative tricks that only compound the problems and add further mistrust to your list of obstacles to overcome.

Open and Closed

Questions can fall into two general categories: closed- and open-ended. As closed-ended questions usually get us into the most trouble, we should start by discussing them. Closed-ended questions allow for a one-word response—yes or no, right or wrong, this way or that. Closed-ended questions are a court favorite and used by lawyers to extract only the information and facts that will help their case. "Were you there on the night in question—yes or no? Did you see my client before the accident—yes or no?" The aggressive attorney doesn't want to hear your reasons for what you did or said—only if you did or said them. He is not looking for an explanation; he wants a fact to use or manipulate.

To return to our analogy of listening, closed-ended questions move you from standing shoulder-to-shoulder to a position to confront your opponent. If you use closed-ended questions about issues in dispute, your discussion can quickly become a head-to-head contest where strength determines the winner. In communicating with your former spouse, asking a series of closed-ended questions will usually antagonize him and shut down his willingness to continue talking.

To be fair, asking closed-ended questions is a great, straightforward way to obtain detailed information and facts: When will you be picking up the children? What time is the soccer practice? When used to learn and understand, closed-ended questions are productive and helpful. However, when you're knee-deep in conflict, closed-ended questions are often misused (or at least perceived) to prove your point. You're trying to make the other parent confess his wrongdoing and validate your position and actions. You are essentially putting him on trial, asking leading questions with loaded answers. Like the attorney examining a witness, you are not interested in understanding the other parent, only in proving your point. No one likes being on trial.

In a co-parenting dispute, seldom is the resolution based on the facts and details. It is rare to have a situation where the dispute over parent-time is simply a matter of not knowing what the schedule is. Each parent has a copy and each knows what it says. What it means, however, may be a different story.

Open-ended questions, on the other hand, are much more effective in identifying issues and concerns and in resolving conflict. These types of questions invite an explanation, experience, and a well thought-out answer. Open-ended questions do not lead to any specific place or point. These are the best ways to exchange information. Examples of open-ended questions are:

"Tell me why . . ."
"What are your thoughts/reasons for . . . ?"
"How would this be a benefit . . . ?"
"Can you give me an example of . . . ?"
"Can you help me understand why . . . ?"

"Could you describe what happened when . . . ?"

"What about . . . is important to you?"

"What might work?"

You can see how the answers to these questions will invite dialogue and discussion of what is bothering the two of you and what is most important. Questions like these invite you to share their stories and explanations, and at the same time, your underlying interests.

Two Questions

It won't surprise you to learn that asking the right type of question at the right time is harder than it looks. How *do* you turn a positional statement, one in which you absolutely cannot agree to, ever compromise with, and isn't even true in your experience, into an interest-based concern you can work with? We would suggest asking the following questions:

- What do you want? and
- What would be different if you had what you want?

These two questions move someone from the "what" he wants to the "why" he wants it. Your positions, or what you say you want, could be quite incompatible—you both want custody of the children, possession of the house, car, or boat, or to never see, speak to, or even have to think about each one. But your interests, or why you want think these things, can often be met with a little work and creativity. Using the above two questions can help.

The first question, "What do you want?" clarifies feelings and brings the other parent's issue and conflict into focus, even if the answer you get is extreme ("I want full custody and control over the children" or "I want you to vanish forever from our lives"). Don't fight or resist the other parent's answers—you asked him what he wanted, after all, and he told you. (If you really didn't want to know, you shouldn't have asked.) Knowing what the other parent wants is the first step in identifying and then resolving the problems that the two of you have.

Once the other parent has told you what he wants, the next question, "What would it be like if you had what you want?" takes the conflict to a new level, maybe for the first time. It is here that you begin to see what it is the other parent needs and is trying to accomplish. Maybe the other parent answered the first question by saying that he wishes he could move away and never see you again. You ask what it would be like if he did. Maybe the answer is that he wouldn't have to see you every other weekend or be forced to talk to you, which usually ends in both of you yelling in front of the children. *Ah-ha!* you think to yourself. *Now we're getting somewhere.* The exchanges are causing stress on your already damaged relationship. Is there another way to exchange the children without face-to-face interaction? Of course there are—lots of them—and away the two of you go.

In our experience, though, you may have to ask the second question more than once to get an answer that reveals the concern. Be careful that it doesn't sound like you are leading the other parent somewhere or fishing for a specific answer. If you have to, and if you can, you may need to move on to a different subject that the other parent wants to discuss, and return to this one later. Be persistent, though. Don't give up on this. Don't accept that the "what" he wants as the end of discussion. It isn't. The other parent may not be ready or trust you enough to share what he *really* wants and what his true concerns are right now. Be patient, and give him every reason to see and trust the new you.

Reframing

So, you've asked the two questions, and know the "what" and "why" of the other parent's concerns, but what do you do with it? The technique of taking a positional statement and turning it into an interest is called a *reframe*. This negotiation tool takes an unusable, usually argumentative statement or accusation, and puts a positive, constructive spin to it. Think of this communication skill as if you were taking an old, cumbersome, and dark painting and putting it in a new frame that shifts the focus of the painting, drawing attention to its lighter scenes or other elements. You don't change anything; you simply shift attention to the more desirable features of it.

Reframing is more than a simple "mirroring" of what the other parent said. It is important that the other parent feels like she's understood instead of just hearing her words repeated back. In the kinds of conflict that sometimes accompany high-conflict divorce, parroting words back with no attempt at understanding them will often be taken as a manipulative trick that spurs on the conflict. A good reframe moves the conversation along, eases anxiety, and helps the other parent (often for the first time) feel understood.

For example, the other parent might say: "You don't care about the children. You're only seeing them because you have to pay child support now." If you just mirror what she has said, you might say back to her, "You think I don't care about the children and that I only want to see them because I pay child support. Is this right?" When you simply mirror what the other parent has said, you run the risk that she will become offended because she believes you are playing games with her, which leads to raising the defenses that much higher. Also, in this example, by mirroring what the other parent has said, you have only strengthened and given validity to her belief and position.

A reframe, however, goes to the heart of the matter, the underlying interest, and what the other parent might be trying to say, but isn't. In this example, if your contact with your children *has* been less than regular and consistent (regardless of the reason), your renewed interest may upset the schedule the other parent and children have become accustomed to. In this case the reframe might sound like, "So stability for you and the children is important to you." You can do a lot to increase stability for the other parent and the children *and* create a liberal and consistent parent-time schedule.

Consider the following statements and possible reframes:

STATEMENT: "You just don't know how to parent."
The REFRAME might be: "You're concerned for our children's welfare."

STATEMENT: "The children don't want to see you anymore, and I'm not going to force them."
The REFRAME might be: "Giving the children a voice is important to you."

STATEMENT: "All you care about is the child support. You don't care if I ever see the children."
The REFRAME might be: "It sounds like you feel like you're not being supported as a parent."

The beauty of the reframe is that if you are wrong, the other parent will be quick to let you know. "No, that's not it at all. All I'm saying is . . ." and the process continues. The other parent may express their real concerns and feelings after only one attempt at a reframe, but more likely you will just get another accusation. Go with it and try to reframe it again. If you're wrong again, apologize and explain that you're just trying to understand what the other parent is saying.

Eventually you will identify the interests driving the other parent's positions and behaviors. It may not happen in one sitting. The conversation and reframe might take place over a couple of days or weeks, and that's okay. Remember, this is not a quick fix. We're talking about building a life-long co-parenting relationship.

These interests are the building blocks of a Win/Win resolution of your conflict. These interests will feel familiar to you, as well. Remember that the two of you share many of these underlying needs and interests. Acknowledge these needs in common, and begin laying the foundation of your new relationship.

Don't Take it Personally

We have touched on this before, but it bears repeating here: don't take what you hear personally. This is easier said than done, we know. Many a parent has suddenly, and forcefully, withdrawn from a mediation session when the other parent begins expressing concerns and fears. These parents are insulted that they have to listen to lies and allegations that they know are not true. They refuse to "sit here and take this" and storm out. A skilled mediator may be able to calm the offended parent down enough to explain the truth of their experience, but sometimes the injury feels too severe. Don't fall victim to this pitfall. Prepare for it. Ask the "What If?" questions and have ways to calm yourself down and keep talking. As the other parent vents and expresses his feelings and frustrations (you asked, remember?), blend with the truth of his experience.

Don't resist, block, or defend against it. If you are strong enough, and have conditioned your life and your response enough, you can acknowledge that the other parent believes that you are a uncaring, self-centered monster without it being true. You can understand what she is feeling without believing it yourself. What is true for her does not make it true for you. You're not on trial here, and neither is the other parent. Remind yourself that you are trying to resolve a conflict, not win a prize.

Being Understood

A chapter on asking questions would be incomplete without some instruction on being understood. Your goal is to find and create a Win/Win resolution to the conflict, and you can't balance the other parent's "win" without presenting and achieving a "win" of your own.

Be Prepared

Just as every Boy Scout adopts and lives by this two-word motto, you need to come to the negotiation table prepared to share and express your own needs and concerns. You cannot expect the other parent will understand your needs and concerns if you don't know exactly what they are, so the first step in being understood is to sort through your own feelings, emotions, and positions, and identify your own interests and motivations.

You must ask yourself the same questions you ask the other parent and be just as persistent with your own answers. You will need to move yourself beyond your own position and discover the underlying concerns driving your actions. Ask yourself what it is you want, and don't fool yourself by pretending it is anything less than what you honestly feel. Then, using the second question, find out *why* you want what you say you want. If, for example, after months or even years of conflict when it comes to sharing and spending time with your children, you decide that enough is enough, and you want full custody of your children. The answer to the first question, "What do you want?" is custody. Now ask yourself the second question, "What would it be like if you had what you want?" Your answers might include that there would be no more missed parent-time, not having to deal with an uncooperative former spouse, you can see to the children's needs that the other parent is neglecting, and you could participate more fully in the children's upbringing and not be considered just a "Disneyland-Dad."

So you might say you want "custody" (your position), but what you really want (your interests) is to spend as much time with your children as possible, care for them, be more involved in their lives, and to love and be loved by them. Where your position (a fight for custody) leaves little room for negotiation, ways to satisfy your interests are only limited by your combined imagination and good faith. As a side note, the other parent may fight your entitlement to custody, but no one can deny your desire to love, spend time with, and be loved by your children. This, you may be sure, is one of the other parent's needs, as well.

Two More Questions

Remember the two questions we shared earlier to change a position or want into an interest or need? Well, there are two more questions that you will need to ask to become better prepared before coming to the negotiation table. You must now ask yourself:

- What have you been willing to do so far to get what you want?
- What *haven't* you been willing to do so far to get what you want?

Asking these questions will give you the new direction you need to resolve old disputes and create new solutions. The first question forces you to evaluate your past behaviors and strategies in dealing with your shared conflict. If, for example, you have had a difficult time speaking to your children on the phone every Tuesday, as it provided for in your decree, your strategy to speak to them might have included calling every ten minutes after the appointed hour, leaving increasingly frustrated voicemails wondering where they are, and demanding that they pick up or call you back. Maybe you have been to court on this issue before, and the judge has ordered that there be no more missed phone calls, but here you are, leaving another message. Asking yourself this first question will test your actions to see if they have been effective.

If what you have tried hasn't worked (and many times it hasn't), asking yourself the second question makes you think outside the proverbial box and list those things that you have not tried yet. Don't limit yourself by saying that you have tried everything and that nothing will work. What *haven't* you tried? Can you ask the other parent to choose a different night or time that is more convenient for him? Is there really something special or critical about Tuesdays? Can you just leave one message asking the other parent to call you back when the children are in bed and asleep? Can you purchase cell phones for the children so that you can reach them anytime and anywhere? If you have tried these things and, in fact, nothing you have ever tried has worked to correct the problem, perhaps you change your weekly contact with the children from phone calls (that haven't been happening anyway) to letter or card writing. If you live far away from the children and your goal is to maintain contact with your children, there are many ways to accomplish this, including letters, sending video or audio cassette tapes back and forth, setting up special email accounts, and the list just goes on and on.

But don't stop there. There is a bigger picture here, a new co-parenting relationship to create with your former spouse. Apply these two questions as you attempt to work things out with the other parent. Once you have uncovered what it is you really want, ask yourself what you have and haven't tried so far to get it. The answer may be hard for you to admit. Most of us know what we don't want and spend a great deal of time and other resources to prevent our worst-case from happening, but do very little to get us nearer to our goal. In fact, many of us don't even know what it is we really want when we are in disagreement with someone.

So ask yourself, what have you tried so far to spend quantity and quality time with your children? What have you done so far to improve the relationship with your former spouse and co-parent? What have you done to reduce the conflict and, at the same time, stand up for your rights and needs? You may have more than a few answers listed here. But answering the next question is crucial to the development of your new co-parenting relationship: What *haven't* you tried yet? Maybe you haven't tried not getting upset, even when you feel you've been wronged. Have you spoken to a counselor or a mediator? Have you picked up a book on how to parent after divorce? Brainstorm as many ideas as you can think of and write them down somewhere. Refer back to them from time to time, and consider each of them as you work on this new relationship.

Expressing It

You may now feel confident about what you have learned about yourself, but before you launch into your needs and underlying interests, remember that the other parent has not had the benefit of seeing your position turn into an interest. A little background and lead-in may be helpful to being understood. This background becomes more of a necessity when your interests are not all in common. But how do you bring up past events or behaviors without the other parent shutting down, raising defenses, or withdrawing from the conversation? The answer could be as easy as ABC.

ABC Statement

One of the most effective means to express a complaint about some action or behavior is using what can we call an ABC or XYZ statement. Now, it is not important what end of the alphabet you start on—what is important is that you include the three elements to this communication tool: the action or behavior (independent of the person), its cause or effect on you, and your feelings or experience as a result—"When A happened, it caused B, and made me feel C."

Take the example of one parent consistently returning the children late. Instead of using a bunch of "you" statements to attack the other parent and his lack of discipline and inability to tell time, your ABC statement might go something like this: "When the children return late, it throws off the night's bedtime routine, and everyone is grouchy and upset all night."

Notice that there is no reference to the other parent in this statement, only the results of the action (the children returning late). The statement was not "When *you* return the children late," only the time the children return. Do you see the skill involved here? A little word here or there can dramatically change the way the conversation goes. You may need to practice you ABC statement several times before all references to the other parent are removed.

This approach to the causes of the conflict separates the person from the problem and, in so doing, reduces his defensiveness and frees up the energy that would have been spent in reacting and defending himself.

Another benefit of the ABC statement is that you are forced to clarify your experience. Your reaction to the children being returned late may be that it just makes you angry. Just saying that it makes you angry offers you and the other parent little to work with. Dig deeper when you find that your experience is limited to a vague emotion. Instead of saying that it makes you angry, ask yourself *why* you are angry. Are you angry because you feel like you are being walked all over, or because you are following the schedule and feel that it is only fair that the other parent do likewise?

It is important here—as in every stage of your divorce and the rebuilding of your life—that you be completely honest with yourself and the other parent. Anything less than an honest experience is nothing but a lousy excuse. If bedtimes go fine regardless of whether the children are returned on time, don't say they aren't. If the result is that you get upset, let them know *how* it upsets you and in what way. Be specific. These are your needs, after all, and you cannot expect the other parent to understand them if you cannot accurately express them.

Mediation

Listening is hard to do, especially at first. If listening were easy, everyone would be doing it. Don't hesitate to enlist the help of a mediator as you start down the pathway toward resolution and peace. Bringing in a neutral third party can ease tensions and give permission for each of you to act in good faith. A mediator can help separate the problems from the people and find creative resolutions. Good direction and suggestions might be refused if it comes from you, but embraced when coming from a mediator. Even if the other parent refuses to go, many mediators offer conflict resolution coaching services. This coaching can help you learn and implement problem-solving skills, and act as a sounding board as you venture out more on your own. They can guide you through difficult times and keep you focused on a true Win/Win resolution.

Summary

We all have the need to be understood, and until we feel like we have been, we cannot lower our defenses enough to listen to an opposing view. So when conflicts arise with your children's other parent, resist the impulse to explain yourself first and convince him that you are right. Listen—really listen—to what he has to say. This will not be easy. You may hear things that offend you and strike at the heart of your very sense of worth, but don't fight back. Blend with the experience, ask questions to really understand why he feels that way, and don't stop until you can see yourself and the conflict through his eyes. When you can understand and reframe the other parent's concerns better than he can express them, then, and only then, can you express your own interests and concerns and hope to be understood as well. Only then are you ready to step onto the mat and engage the other parent in negotiation.

Just Do It

If listening is the most important element of good communication, then asking questions is a close second. It is one thing to simply sit there and listen to what the other parent is saying, but it is another skill entirely to ask questions to know why he or she believes that way. Asking questions is scary, partly because it opens you up and makes you vulnerable to further attacks, and partly because of the answers you might hear. But this fear goes away with every question asked. You come to realize that asking questions is the only way you can reach the heart of the disagreement and from there take the steps necessary to resolve it.

60

1. Before you move on to the next chapter, choose a subject that you and the other parent might disagree on and ask yourself the four questions listed we emphasized earlier. Write down your answers.

    a. What do you want?

    b. What would be different if you had what you want?

    c. What have you been willing to do to get what you want?

    d. What haven't you been willing to do so far to get what you want?

2. Practice reframing some of your own complaints, removing any reference to anyone else. Do you see how clearer the issues become?

3. Do you ask questions to get to the underlying interests, or do you take the position for what it is?

4. Do you *really* know what you want? Have you practiced expressing it before?

5. Have you practiced the ABC statements? Can you express your concerns and complaints without any reference at all to your former spouse?

7

Principled Negotiation 101

With great power comes great responsibility. The principles and techniques presented here may give you an advantage over your former spouse when it comes to negotiating matters of your divorce. We cannot stress enough the warning that this knowledge gives you power and that power must not be used to manipulate your former spouse into getting a bigger piece of the pie for yourself. It will, no doubt, be tempting to use this upper hand to get what you want and, perhaps, exact a little well-deserved revenge. Resist this temptation. Whatever else you do, don't. Don't. Don't.

When Forever Doesn't Last is not about getting what you want right now. You are going to be family and working together for a very long time. It is of supreme importance that your negotiations be conducted with only the highest of integrity. You may not have started the divorce, you may not have even wanted it, but it may now be up to you to take the higher road, apply the teachings of the Master, and resolve it in a way that will bring peace and harmony back your lives.

Go to the Mountain

Throughout history, mountains have played an important, yet silent, role in the spiritual, ethical, and legal development of mankind. Many of history's greatest leaders and thinkers have fled to the mountains receive inspiration and guidance. Men and women of God have been found seeking solitude and wisdom at higher elevations: Abraham was told that he was to be the father of nations on a mountain east of Beth-el, and it was on the mountain of Moriah that he was commanded to offer up his son Isaac; Moses ascended Mount Sinai to receive the Ten Commandments; the Brother of Jared went up the mountain to inquire of the Lord; and Nephi was caught away in the Spirit of the Lord into an exceeding high mountain. When he began his earthly ministry, Jesus Christ went up into a mountain to meditate and receive light and knowledge, it was on the Mount of Olives that angels and heavenly messengers later

> **The significant problems we face cannot be solved at the same level of thinking we were at when we created them.**
> —Albert Einstein

instructed him, and it was upon a sacred mount at Jerusalem that the ultimate sacrifice was made on behalf of all mankind.

Why go the mountains? What is so special about them? Perhaps it is because they are the meeting place between heaven and earth, and by standing upon a mountain's peak, you feel closer to deity and can hear more clearly celestial instruction. Or by ascending one's height, you rise above the valley floor and the world in which you live and labor, day after day, and are able to see more, much further than you could before. Looking down on the world in which you live gives you a different and broader perspective. From the mountain's top you can see patterns in the land, the winding rivers, and planned pathways around the (now) small rocks, hills, and other obstacles. From the top of the mountain you can see borders of the city in which you live and beyond. What you thought was big turns out to be very small compared to the surrounding countryside, and a sense of peace settles in when you see the whole picture. It is on the mountain that you can rise above the conflict and chaos, even if for only a moment, and see the beginning from the end, the alpha from the omega—in short, you can see the Big Picture.

The Big Picture

So what is this *bigger* picture that you are supposed to see from atop "the mountain"? For our purposes here, it needs to include the goal to develop a working co-parenting relationship with your former spouse. You should see that, at least on one level, your divorce is little more than a restructuring of the family. You and your former spouse are no longer husband and wife, but you continue

> **A pebble held close to the eye appears to be a gigantic obstacle. Cast on the ground, it is seen in perspective.**
> – Richard G. Scott

to be your children's mother and father. From the mountain, you will see that the two of you need to come to an understanding and acceptance of each other's strengths and weaknesses and use them to complement each other as you each do the best

you can for your children. From this elevated height, you can see that your children need both of you in their lives now and forever. It will take both of you to make them whole and complete, seeing that they may require special attention and cooperation to survive the decision to divorce.

From the mountain you will see not only your goals and hopes for the future, but if you've listened, the other parent's, as well. You will know what concerns he has and what needs he possesses, and you can begin to develop a plan and chart a path where both of you may journey in peace.

One Step at a Time

From the mountain you will notice the distances you have to travel to get from where you are to where you would like to be. Plan your steps accordingly. You will see that a good, strong, healthy co-parenting arrangement needs to include the discussion of general parenting philosophies, parent-time schedules, financial and emotional support for the children, religious and moral training, and parenting responsibilities, to name only a few.

Do not deceive yourself into thinking you can do this all at once. It is unrealistic to hope that one discussion or mediation session, will have the power to resolve and unravel months or years of conflict. You may be tired of hearing this, but there is no quick fix—no shortcut to a strong relationship.

A Test of Conditioning

Before we present the negotiation and mediation steps and procedures, we need to pause and say that it is here, putting into practice these next few skills and communication tools, that you will rely on and use every bit of training and conditioning that we discussed in Chapter Two. Because they are essential to your safety and success during the negotiations, let's review them here.

A "Relaxed" Lifestyle. Does your lifestyle allow you the freedom to move about and adapt and adjust to the creation of a new co-parenting relationship? If every hour of every day is committed to some activity or another, your ability to move freely as you negotiate will be limited. Other limitations to your freedom to do what is best in working toward an agreement often come in the way of expectations of family or friends. We will discuss later how best to manage your friends and family and *help* them to really help you during this time of your life. For now, you must be in a position to set appropriate boundaries and limit their influence on a centered and Win/Win focus. Anyway you do it, see that your life is flexible and loose enough to accommodate moving through the negotiation process.

Being Flexible. It does no good to have a relaxed lifestyle if you, yourself, are not flexible, as well. Insisting on your solutions to the problems and diverting energy to being stiff and "playing hardball" only hurts your chance of reaching a lasting agreement. To be flexible during your negotiations means focusing, and refocusing, on interests and needs, and looking for other, more creative ways to meet them. Flexibility means recognizing and knowing the differences between your own positions and interests. Being flexible will make it easier to meet the other parent's needs and will help them respond in kind.

Falling and Rolling. We will all be surprised and blindsided from time to time. Knowing how to fall and roll correctly will prevent injury and get you back on your feet and rebalanced quickly. If, during the course of the negotiation, the other parent expresses unfounded concerns about your ability to parent and insists that your parent-time be supervised, will you fall and roll with the concern and re-center yourself to find balance and continue working toward a constructive resolution? Prepare yourself with answers and plans for a wide range of "What If?" questions. Falling and rolling with a concern, instead of resisting and risking further injury to your struggling co-parenting relationship, will keep you safe during the process.

Are You Strong Enough? As you prepare to enter the negotiations with your former spouse, one of your greatest assets is to know your strengths and weaknesses. Identifying existing strengths and creating new ones provides you with greater balance as you interact with the other parent. We have seen many parents who believe that the only leverage they have is to deny the other parent access to the children or withhold child support payments. This is a heavy blow to the other parent and often not an equal punishment for her offense. But if you have no other means to exert yourself, and few effective communication tools to work through problems and conflict, then you may feel forced to resort to these kinds of hardball tactics. Perhaps you can find new strength in the stability of your new life, your new job, friends, your refusal to play common and destructive divorce games, or your resolve to do what is right every time.

Speed and Timing. The key to acting quickly is anticipation. Walking through a dark parking garage, you study your surroundings, observing where the light falls, noticing where danger might lurk, and then taking the safer course. If you have practiced handling the problems that might come your way, you can act in a productive manner almost without thinking about it. It becomes instinctual. Being prepared ahead of time by charting out where conflict is likely to come from in your negotiations allows you to maintain control over the process and keep the negotiations moving forward toward a Win/Win solution.

The Words You Use. There are phrases and terms used by the domestic legal field that invoke a defensive and negative response in parents. Words like *custody* and *visitation* perpetuate the false assumption that divorce is a contest and that there needs to be a winner and a loser. These words, and many others, need to be avoided in your conversations with the other parent. Instead, talk about the children's residence and their access to both parents. Assessing fault or blame is a surefire way to shut down communications between you and the other parent. Any reference to fault or blame is usually past-oriented and not future-focused. Solutions are found in the future.

Centering. One last word on being centered and balanced before we proceed. Keep close to your center. Whether it is your newfound sense of worth, the love you have for your children, or a new or renewed faith in God—let nothing move you from your center. It is here that you are at your strongest and where you are most at peace. The further you are lured or pulled from your center, the weaker and more off balance you become. Do not be tricked or coerced into moving from your center and circle of strength. It will not be easy, but take counsel from the fable of the oak tree and the reed—you can stay rooted and at the same time bend and move with the raging storm. This is what it means to be centered.

The Not-So-Magic Formula

So if you are ready, we will begin your negotiating training. At the core of this mediation process are four steps that, when taken in order, will lead you down the path of conflict resolution. These steps have been taken by millions before you and will be used by yet millions more. Every divorce mediator presents this formula and teaches his clients these simple steps to move difficult conversations forward.

At the outset, we should bring up two questions that are often asked: "Does this process really work?" and "Can I actually use them?" To both questions we answer: U-BET:

Understand
Brainstorm
Evaluate
Test

Understand

It is not an accident that an entire chapter was dedicated to the art and practice of listening. Listening to the other parent as he expresses his concerns and complaints, and then asking the right questions until you understand his point of view is the first, and most important, step to effective and constructive negotiations. There is no shortcut or substitute. You cannot skip the listening and jump right into the mediation process and hope to create anything other than distrust and continued conflict.

Brainstorm

Understanding the other parent's needs and concerns is only the first step toward resolving the conflict and problems. It does no good to understand the other parent's concerns and not want to or know how to resolve them. Where do you begin? What can you possibly do differently this time when all other past attempts have failed? As you ask yourself these kinds of questions, remember that you do not have all the answers. It is *not* your job alone to meet everyone's needs and resolve everyone's concerns. Don't take this the wrong way, but you *can't* solve it all by yourself.

Divorced parents in conflict often become stuck and break off their attempts to resolve some problem or dispute. They see no other option than to go to court and let a judge decide. It is this "no other option" the can lead to further problems and compound the conflict. One of the real benefits of using a mediator is his ability, as a neutral third-party, to stimulate ongoing discussions and generate possible ideas for resolution. This brainstorming of ideas is crucial to the process. It is often a determining factor of whether issues are resolved. If you are proceeding on your own, it is up to you to get this brainstorming session underway.

> **Nothing is more dangerous than an idea when it is the only one you have.**
> —Emilie Chartier

The purpose of brainstorming is to generate as many ideas for possible resolution as possible. For many of us, the very nature of our conflict prevents us from thinking of creative ways to solve our problems. Instead, the conflict strengthens our belief that a strong-arm, hardball tactic is required. After all, we've tried everything else before and nothing has worked, right? Wrong.

Before brainstorming with the other parent, you need to follow two rules to make your time successful. You may want to share them with the other parent before you start.

Rule One: **Any idea, no matter how crazy, should be shared.** If it crosses your mind, list it on the board. If it is humanly and physically possible, throw it out there. No idea is too crazy or bizarre not to be included. It is often the most outlandish ideas that serve as a basis or starting point for the future agreement. Possible solutions to the problems often begin with the words, "Well, it's not like we could just . . ." Hidden within the doubt is often the seed from which an agreement could grow. Include every idea. Keep a list. Write them down, no matter how strange or unworkable they might appear to be.

It is natural to list all of the ideas that won't work. Many of us have no problems telling someone what we *don't* want or what *won't* work, but have a much harder time expressing what *will*. We are quick to find fault with the cause of the problem, but usually spend very little time thinking of possible resolutions. Brainstorming fights the almost natural instinct to limit our options, and instead opens up a new world of possibilities. You know that proverbial "box" we find ourselves in most of the time? Brainstorming is one of the quickest ways out of it.

Rule Two: **No idea can be criticized or dismissed from the list.** Include them all, even if you know that there is no way you'll ever go along with it. The other parent may suggest extreme solutions to end the conflict, like having you give up all rights to your children and disappearing forever from their lives. You would never in a million years consider leaving your children, but it is an idea and needs to be included on the list. You may even want to include ideas that others have shared with you in the past. Who knows, your mother's great-aunt may have mentioned an idea that worked during her divorce that might work here with you. Stranger things have happened.

Evaluate

Once every conceivable idea has been shared and listed, it is time to organize and evaluate what the two of you came up with. John Haynes, the pioneer of domestic mediation and mentor to divorce mediators all over the world, suggests that you list them into one of four categories: highly possible, possible, unlikely, and impossible. The criteria for each of these lists are the ability to meet *both* of your needs.

Take the necessary time to review and explore every suggestion, even the inflammatory ones. It is important that credit be given to every idea listed—the good, the bad, and the ugly. Consider each one carefully and apply it to your identified needs and interests. Fight the urge to rate all of *your* ideas as possible or highly possible, while discounting the other parent's. Could her ideas work? What are the drawbacks? Are they obvious, or do you need to spend some time discussing them? The ideas that do not address or meet both of your interests and needs should be listed under the unlikely or impossible tables. Be careful that you do not begin by criticizing the other parent's ideas, even if they are clearly impossible. If you have identified your individual and shared needs and interests and have written them down somewhere, you can ask, "Does this (idea or proposed solution) help us meet our goals of (whatever the two of you have listed)?" The bad ones will be apparent, and the good ones will begin to emerge. Remember, though, now is not the time for decisions, only evaluations.

Now, what's to stop the other parent from automatically throwing every single one of you ideas into the impossible list, and insisting that her ideas are the only good ones? Nothing. This is likely to happen to you at first. But we would hope that if she has been listened to and feels understood by you, the ideas you both generate would seem of value. It may be a test of your sincerity to really work with the other parent, or it may be a genuine difficulty seeing any other possible solution. In either case, this may be the time for you to return to the issues and interests already identified, and dig a little further, asking questions to discover any additional concerns or needs that were not shared before.

Don't expect full cooperation from the other parent—especially at first. Remember, it may take them a little while to trust the "new" you. That's okay. You are not changing for the other parent's benefit—you are changing for yours. Remain centered and balanced through this stage of the process, and be sincere in your quest to find a Win/Win agreements to your problems.

Test

Once you have evaluated the ideas and placed them in one of the four categories, your next step is to put them to the test. It is important that you only test the possible and highly possible ideas. It is easy to get caught up in the frenzy of explaining why the unlikely and impossible ones won't work. Don't. You both know they won't work, so leave it at that. You can disregard the impossible ideas, and put the unlikely ones on the shelf for now. Your thoughts should be positive and focused on the future.

Begin by exploring the highly possible ideas first, and apply them to you situation. Play the "What If?" game and carry it through to the end. Put each idea through a reality test and see what it looks like. Take turns being the devil's advocate as you determine whether the proposed solution will actually work. Start testing your own first, looking for flaws in your own ideas and logic. The other parent will see this, and it will be easier to put hers to the test as well.

Don't forget the children as you test your ideas. How are they likely to respond and cope with your new plans? Does your potential agreement have the children waking up at five in the morning so you can drop them off before you go to work? Or is the plan to pick up the children after eleven at night once you get off working the swing shift? You know your children better than anyone. Will these schedules work for them and help them adjust to your divorce and separation, too? Are they old enough to be given a voice, or are they still young enough to trust you to meet their needs in your agreement?

It is important to remember that the best agreement on paper may not actually work in the real world. Now is the time to put your ideas into as many hypothetical scenarios as you can think of. You may even want to pause and have a mini-brainstorming session. Don't hold anything back. It is much easier to consider and anticipate potential problems before your plan is implemented. If something could affect the agreement, bring it up and deal with it—don't put it off, hoping it never comes up.

Summary of U-BET

The U-BET formula does work. It is not easy, though, and will take time to practice and perfect. Listening to understand is one of the hardest tasks you will ever do, especially when there are opposing views, different experiences, and high emotions. It is not natural to shut up and really hear what the other parent is saying, but there is no way to skip this step on the journey to repair or rebuild a lasting and effective co-parenting relationship. Once each of you have heard and understood each other, brainstorming as many possible ideas for resolution is crucial. Your first ideas and suggestions often resemble your positions and will not be accepted by the other parent. Make a list and include every idea shared, possible or not, then evaluate them using your interests and needs as the standard to which they are applied. Then put the ones you both think might work to the test, looking for problems down the road. In the end, it is likely you will have found a resolution that addresses each of your concerns and meets both of your needs.

Summary

Once you have listened to the concerns of the other parent and have clearly identified her needs, it will take real skill, and maybe even a little luck, to blend those needs with your own and find ways to meet them. To accomplish this, you will need to rise above the conflict. Go to your mountain to gain a broader perspective, and see your place and time in the big picture. With this newfound inspiration, you can generate ideas freely, evaluate them, and put them to the test. (Can you do this? U-BET you can.) Be patient and take breaks as necessary. No one is at his best when he is tired and frustrated. You will make mistakes. Learn from them, and then try again. Cut yourself some slack, don't get discouraged, move with strength and confidence from your center, and to quote Winston Churchill, "Never, never, never give up."

Just Do It

Before you move on, take a minute and give yourself a good reality check. Make sure you understand the mediation concepts and U-BET process.

1. Do you have a crystal-clear big picture yet?
2. Take a minute or two to identify some of the small steps you can take toward the reaching your big picture goals.
3. What do you want your co-parenting relationship to look like one year from now? Five years? Ten years?
4. If you are trying to resolve a current problem, have you spent the necessary time to listen to the other parent and her point of view? Have you brainstormed at least a dozen *possible* solutions? Which ones could work? Look ahead a year—is there anything that might come up to disrupt your ideas?

8
Hitting the Proverbial "Brick Wall"

The U-BET process is at the heart of every mediation session and has been proved successful in cases more numerous to count. But negotiations do not always go smoothly—especially over matters concerning where children will reside and how much time they will spend with each parent. In fact, unless you already have a strong co-parenting relationship in place, they seldom do. What can you do when you've tried the above steps and put the U-BET formula into practice, and you still have not resolved your disputes?

Impasse

What if the other parent insists on using unfair and confrontational tactics to get his way, and despite all of your efforts and good faith, you find yourselves at a deadlock, stalemate, or what is called an *impasse?* A mediator has an entire toolbox of skills and techniques devoted to breaking deadlocks and moving the negotiations forward, many of which you can use as you work toward a Win/Win resolution to your co-parenting difficulties. The remainder of this chapter is dedicated to teaching you some of those skills.

We offer three levels of techniques to help jump-start a stalled negotiation. The first level focuses on additional things *you* can do to overcome the difficulties that may have led to the breakdown. The second-level suggestions are stronger and more interactive to help identify exactly where the impasse occurred and to generate alternatives to resolve these specific concerns. The third level contains the most direct and confrontational techniques we have to offer. This level's steps are reserved for the really difficult negotiations and should be used only after the first two levels have been attempted.

Level One

When the stakes or emotions are high, almost every negotiation will experience impasse at one time or another. This is common; in fact, when you run into a brick wall there is a good chance that you are on the right track and making real progress. It is easier to just pretend to go along with something instead of standing up for some issue you or the other parent feels strongly about. The following three suggestions may help you break the impasse and move toward an agreement.

Ask Yourself . . .

Ask yourself two questions: "What can you offer the other parent to move them closer to your ideas?" and "What could the other parent offer you to move you closer to theirs?" Take a break and think about the answers you come up with. You may want to share these questions and your answers with the other parent. This is not a manipulation or trick—you are genuinely trying to understand her needs and give her what she needs to come to a and Win/Win solution to the problems at hand. Listen closely to what she says. You may learn that you have misunderstood her interests and needs, or you may be (for the first time) helping the other parent identify what it is she really needs. At the very least, it will generate further dialogue (even if it is just to tell you how wrong and far off the mark your thinking is).

Take a Hike

Return to the mountain and share your view with the other parent. Focus on the future, and place a long-term, big-picture value on the issue in dispute. You or the other parent may want or need what is in dispute now, but is it really worth it in the end? Invite the other parent to explain why she feels so strongly about her idea or yours, and listen closely. Hidden in their answer may just be the solution to the problem. Keep your focus on the future and explore the benefits each of you sees along your different paths.

Reschedule

If you and the other parent are stuck over some issue, you may want to ask if it is okay to postpone discussing it. Write it down and post it somewhere, so it's not forgotten, and move on to another issue. If the other parent objects, don't force it. Instead, explain that you are just suggesting for each of you to give it more thought. There is no quick fix to parenting and relationship issues. We caution you to use this tool carefully. Don't pass up more than one or two issues at a time. If you have too many tough issues stacking up in your "later" box, finding an agreement for them may seem overwhelming and further sabotage your attempts to work together in dispute resolution.

Level Two

The second level of techniques includes presenting questions and scenarios to break down the issues in dispute and uncover exactly where the dispute rests. Here you will take listening, questions, and reframing to a new level and with a slightly different emphasis. You will need to dig deeper as you try to understand not only the other parent's underlying interests, but your own as well. This may be a maiden voyage into possibly unfamiliar and uncomfortable lands. Your patience will be tested on this level as will your desire to reach a mutually satisfying co-parenting arrangement. So, if we haven't scared you away, let's begin.

Break It Down

We've all heard the children's joke that asks, "How do you eat an elephant?" The answer: one bite at a time. There is wisdom in this answer. Seen in its entirety, your problems can appear too big for just the two of you to resolve. You may believe that someone else, stronger and with more power, like an attorney or a judge, is needed to intervene and solve your problems. But if you can break the problems down into its parts, big things suddenly become small.

Let's take one of the biggest impasses common to divorce: custody. No issue in divorce is found where emotions run higher or where more money is spent than on seeking and fighting for custody of the children. The courts have set it up as a Win/Lose situation—either you win, and are awarded custody, or the other parent does. You might think that this in some way determines who is the better parent or loves the children more. But if you break down the Win/Lose determination of custody, you can address each of its components and begin identifying what part of having custody means so much to you. Is it important to have the children come to your home after school? Is it your involvement in homework or after-school activities that mean so much? Is it more important to you to make the day-to-day or the big decisions in the children's lives? This would be an excellent time to repeat the question, "What would it be like if you got what you wanted?" Pay close attention to the answers you both come up with. If you both want to spend time with the children at night or help with homework, remind yourselves that parenting responsibilities and opportunities are not an all-or-nothing arrangement. There are twenty-four hours in a day, seven days a week, fifty-two weeks in a year—you have plenty of time to share.

"What If . . ."

Many mediators find it helpful to play the "What If?" game, presenting each conflicting solution and playing it out a few steps to see how it looks. What if the children lived with you? How might your relationship with them be strengthened? What if they lived with the other parent? It is natural to have some level of fear of the "What if" question. Often, it is the first time that the parents have considered what would happen if the opposite of what they wanted, thought was right, and fair happened. Don't push the answer. Again, the burden will fall to your shoulders to help identify exactly where the problems are and to move the dialogue forward.

Switching Shoes

The last communication and negotiation technique for the second level is called Switching Shoes. Again, we would advise that you use this tool with caution, because it has the potential to erupt into a fireworks show worthy of a Fourth of July celebration. Switching shoes means you switch circumstances with the other parent. Ask what the other parent would need or expect from you if the shoe was on the other foot. For example, let's say the other parent made it difficult for you to have access to your children. You might say, "If the children were living primarily with me and you had some difficulty seeing them when you were entitled to, what would expect me to do to help you?" The answer will likely have a concern about your behavior that will join the list of interests that need to be resolved.

Our caution with this tool lies in how you "paint" the other parent and their actions. Do not include motives for their actions or accusations. ("If the children were living with me *and I was violating the order of the court . . .*) Just keep to your experience and truth, and let the other parent answer your question in whatever way she chooses.

Level Three

If you get to this level in your attempts to resolve your differences, you may be tempted to pack it up and go to court (or give up, give in, or show him or her). To this we say that you may be right. But before you choose to break off the negotiations, let us explore some of your options at this level of impasse.

As we move carefully into this next section, we assume that all previous steps and negotiation tools have been used to the best of your ability and the other two levels were completed or at least taken into consideration. If you have tried John Haynes' two questions, broken down the issues in dispute, asked "What if?" questions to uncover the real concerns, Switched Shoes, and you are still no closer to reaching an agreement, a change in approach may be in order.

At this level, we will touch on three techniques designed to counter a stonewalled negotiation and move it from inactivity while still proceeding with integrity. Of all of the skills we will share in this book, these will feel like they do not belong here, being the strongest and most direct. These three tools include know and clarify what your best alternatives are if this process doesn't work; make small concessions and trade-offs; and, finally, leave the table constructively.

Your BATNA

What alternatives do you have? The very fact that someone voluntarily enters into a negotiation implies that she has alternatives to talking to you. Mediating because you "have no other choice" is not mediation at all—it is simply a delay of the inevitability of giving in to the other party's demands or taking the matter before a judge to decide. Having a choice of whether you negotiate gives you strength in the process. You can choose between what is being offered and what you could get elsewhere. These alternatives are what Fisher and Ury, in their book *Getting to Yes*, call your BATNA, or Best Alternative To a Negotiated Agreement.

In every negotiation, the stronger your BATNA, the more control you have during the negotiation process. Your BATNA is your walk-away alternative. It is your bottom-line figure, the minimum that you'll accept. Agreeing to anything less would be just foolish. A skilled mediator will prepare each party by helping them explore their other options and alternatives to reaching an agreement at the mediation. Negotiating under pressure only invites regret, future non-compliance, and more problems.

Without calling it such, you have been developing your BATNA since Chapter Two when you began your preparation for your new life. There you began to prepare for the rough waters that would surely surface in your journey. There you learned how to be flexible and how to fall and roll properly to avoid injury. It is here that we put that conditioning into practice as your BATNA.

What are your options? What alternatives do you have that will meet your needs, or at least cut your losses, if you decide to withdraw from the process? To know what your BATNA is, you first need to understand and clearly identify what your bottom line, or jumping-off point, is. For example, if you are at an impasse over how much time the children will spend with each parent (a parent-time or visitation schedule), it would be helpful for you to know what the minimum guidelines are for your state or jurisdiction. Any agreement to less time than this is not in your best interest unless it has some other benefit.

A large part of your BATNA is being aware of and realistic regarding your resources. Sure, you *could* go to court and have the judge designate you as the primary physical custodian of your children, but do you have the legal training to go before the court and make your case? Do you have the money to hire an attorney to do it for you? If the answer to these questions is no, then you need to consider whether going to court is *really* an option available to you. Many parents quit the mediation process with the declaration that they will see the other parent in court, only to wind up frustrated that they can't even get the help to file a motion or schedule a court hearing on their own. Or they learn that they will have to pick up an extra shift a week for the next year to come up with the attorney's upfront retainer. These parents are unable to move forward, have burned bridges, and now can't go back to the mediation table. For most parents experiencing problems in their post-divorce relationship, mediation or some other alternative to going to court is really their best chance for real and lasting resolution.

So, consider the cost and resources available to you and know your alternatives—you still have room to negotiate a better deal with the other parent. If you choose to stay in this process with the other parent, consider the next technique.

The Trade-off

When most people think of negotiating, they think compromising or, as we will call it, the "Trade-off." The rules are deceptively simple: I'll give you this if you will give me that. Although the Trade-off results in each of you losing some of what is important to you, it may be necessary as you start your journey of working together as co-parents. Just as you can't run before you can walk, you need to meet halfway in a compromise before you can extend your good faith and adopt a Win/Win philosophy and practice. Where trust and cooperation are low, the Trade-off may be the first step on your way to an empathetic and effective co-parenting relationship.

The Trade-off is also useful, for example, when it is not practical for you, or your children, to divide something—like a holiday. There are, after all, only so many hours in a day. It may be best to alternate and trade certain holidays every year. Oh, sure, if it were up to you, the children would spend every Christmas Eve and Christmas morning with you, as well as every major holiday and other special times, but that is not possible nor is it generally best for your children.

If you engage in the Trade-off to jumpstart a stalled negotiation, remember to ask yourself if it is better than your BATNA. You don't want to trade a dollar for ninety cents (unless you really need the change), and you don't want to trade what is truly important to you for second best, just to reach an agreement. Also, the Trade-off should go at least partway toward meeting both of your interests and needs.

The Trade-off is dangerous, however, because it invites exaggerated claims and inflated values. Priorities go by the wayside as little and insignificant things take their place alongside big and important things. Too often in the Trade-off, President's Day becomes equally as important as Christmas. It may fall on you to regulate the value of each "item" in trade and question its worth.

Concessions

The last technique to break a stubborn impasse is to offer small concessions in exchange for compliance to a future agreement. Now, we know that the very idea of giving in to the other parent might raise your defensiveness and give you a knot in your stomach. Look at your BATNA. If you have another path available to you, now might be the time to take it. But if you don't, offering something of value (and in dispute) to the other parent in good faith, without expectations that he respond in kind, may be enough to break your deadlock and change the direction and momentum of the negotiations.

But before you start giving away your world, we offer a few guidelines and cautions. First, use this sparingly, and by sparingly we mean once. You are buying your agreement. You do not want to communicate to the other parent that if he holds out long enough that you will eventually give in and give him everything he wants.

Second, any concession you offer to the other parent needs to be made with the understanding that it is a one-time offer. Be clear on the terms of your small concession. You may be willing to go along with it this time, but never again. And then if it does happen again, you must stick to your word and not concede again. Many times it is a test. You'll recall that one of the definitions of integrity is saying what you'll do and doing what you say. A repeat of circumstances is most likely a test of your integrity, and you need to pass this test. Again, check the concession (and its consequences) against your BATNA. Does what you're doing make sense? If it does, don't hesitate to apply this technique to your impasse and see what happens.

Move On

In the end, and on some heavily contested issues, an agreement may not be possible. The prior relationship may be too damaged, and the reserves of trust and good faith have been depleted. In these circumstances you may find yourself stepping away from the negotiation table, but we emphasize that you should always be willing to discuss the issues again, come back to the table, and welcome another attempt to work together to build a better co-parenting relationship. However, if there appears to be no working through some issue or another, the best thing you can do is walk away from the negotiating table and go with one of your alternatives. Before you do, consider two things first.

Don't "Kitchen Sink"

If you have applied the techniques presented here to your disagreements and sources of conflict, it is likely that you have worked out many of your points of concern and met many (if not most) of your needs along the way.

Unfortunately, it is common for parents in dispute to focus on the one or two issues that remain in dispute, making these issues "deal-breakers." This Win/Lose, all-or-nothing approach scuttles all the hard work and progress made up to that point and causes even more conflict and a greater sense of failure than when you started the process. If you are going to terminate the process, be clear on what issues you believe have been resolved and what issues are still in disagreement. Resist the urge to throw everything, including the kitchen sink, out the window because you were at an impasse over one or two issues. It's okay. You can "agree to disagree" on some issues.

Even if the other parent walks out on you first and you can't verbally cover your progress and disagreements, it may be well worth your time to draft up your understanding of what issues were resolved and what issues still need resolution. If you do, be sure to phrase the outstanding issue(s) as a mutual concern. For example, don't say that "Sally wants custody," rather, say that the issue is "Where the children's primary residence will be." You might ask what the difference is in these two statements; they are both saying the same thing. The difference is in how it's said. The first statement sets you up for a Win/Lose, either/or decision, whereas the second one provides the opportunity to be creative in finding a resolution.

"What's Next?"

Crucial to ending a principled negotiation is to plan your alternatives and discuss what is going to happen next. Now, be careful that what you say is not conveyed as a threat ("I'll see you in court!") but as an exploration of what is likely to happen ("Looks like we need to let a judge decide this for us"). Where possible, plan your alternatives together. You may need to contact the other parent later (especially if your last meeting ended in fireworks, and one or both of you stormed away) and ask him what is next. Even if the other parent doesn't want to talk to you, you can still share your plan for resolution. Maybe court is the next step, and if it is, you should let the other parent know what you plan to do. Again, if you are centered and have a balanced perspective, it will be your responsibility to see that injury does not come to the other parent. It does no good (and will only serve to hurt your former spouse and damage any hope you might have for a future co-parenting relationship) if you were to speak to an aggressive attorney who then blindsides the other parent with an Order to Show Cause for Contempt. Don't do it. Instead, you should let the other parent know that you are going to get some advice from an attorney on how to resolve said issues, and then decide what to do from there.

You might suggest the use of divorced parenting education, mediation, or arbitration. If the issue is the value of a business or retirement pension, you may want to speak to an accountant to get an objective evaluation. If your area of dispute involves the children, you may choose to jointly speak to a therapist or custody evaluator. All too often, people make the mistake of running to court instead of working toward resolving their own issues. Think about it, an attorney or judge doesn't know the value of your business, or what is in the best interest of you children. They are going to require that experts be called in to offer their opinions and recommendations. Why not skip the (expensive) middlemen and go directly to the experts to get the help you need? Then you can return to the negotiation table and pick up the process where you left off.

"Be Still"

Before we leave the subject of negotiation skills and techniques, we want to let you in on a little secret: sometimes the best thing you can say to help move the negotiations forward is to say nothing at all. Silence is a powerful communication and negotiation tool that is often overlooked. Silence allows for deeper consideration of what is being discussed and gives time for you to return to the mountain to see your options. It can allow an attack or an attempt to derail the negotiations to pass by without causing damage to you or the resolution process. And if the other parent fights and objects to every word and suggestion, silence gives them nothing to resist.

Most of us, however, are uncomfortable with silence. The void caused by silence almost screams to be filled. Silence is oftentimes perceived as rude; those around us assume that we are depressed or angry. When there is a lull in the conversation, especially a conflicted or emotionally charged one, we feel an overpowering urge to say *something*. Anything is better than nothing, right? Not always. It is important that you become a friend to silence and be comfortable in its presence. When you are centered, you will better find the quiet eye of the hurricane that is your divorce conflict raging all around you.

When we say that silence can be used as a great negotiating tool, we do not mean that you give the other parent the cold shoulder or "silent treatment." Using silence means pausing after asking a question and waiting for a thoughtful response. It means not responding immediately to an unreasonable statement or demand. It means having patience while an offer is thought through and carefully considered. It means not repeating your last question, thinking or pretending that the other parent simply did not hear you, and forcing an immediate, and often negative, answer. When used at the right time, and in the right way, silence can help you move toward a mutually satisfying and Win/Win agreement.

Consider the following example. When you ask what a fair division of your children's off-track time from school would be, and the other parent quickly responds that it is not negotiable and that the children will be staying with her, don't take the bait and lash out with statutes, laws, your rights, and how she is unrealistic and impossible. Instead, wait patiently before you answer. You asked what would be fair, not what they would like to see happen, and you need to be comfortable waiting until you hear a reasonable answer. A warning here: it is dangerous to tell the other parent why you are responding with silence. For you to say, "I'm not going to respond because I am waiting for you to answer the question I asked," will most assuredly cause the other parent to stick to her answer as a matter of principle. Just wait a moment or two, and see what happens.

If the other parent is uncomfortable with the silence and turns the question back on you, asking what you think would be fair, respond with a Win/Win proposal that takes into consideration his needs as well as your own, and then wait for his reply. Filling the void with excessive talk and justifying what you think is fair might be perceived as an act of desperation and raise suspicions. In these situations, less is more. Answering briefly and clearly communicates that your answer is strong enough to stand on its own. If you are asked clarifying questions, answer them, of course. But do not be pulled or tricked into doing all of the talking. Be still, and let silence work its power on the negotiations.

Summary

Bear in mind that your early (or even later) attempts to resolve your conflict may not produce the miraculous results you want right away. We've said it before, and we'll no doubt say it again, *When Forever Doesn't Last* is not a quick fix formula for getting what you want. It's about co-parenting relationship and doing the right thing—not because of the promise of favorable results, but because it is the right thing to do. Some issues will be resolved quickly, others will take a great deal of time and effort to work through, and a few gaps will not be bridged. In these cases, knowing the right way to withdraw from the process and proceed along some other path can still serve to build and strengthen your co-parenting relationship.

Just Do It

Hitting that proverbial "brick wall" is evitable and can be frustrating and discouraging. But even walking away (as opposed to staying in the fight) can serve to diffuse the situation and ultimately resolve the conflict. Impasse can be a real test of character and commitment. Consider the following:

1. Answer honestly: How have you handled impasse before? Did it work? Would one of the suggestions presented here do better?
2. Do you know what your options really are? Do they feel like viable options or just giving up?
3. What is your comfort level with silence? Can you endure it? Can you use it?

SECTION IV

SUBSTANCE

"Can two walk together, except they be agreed?"

—Amos 3:3

9

The Agreement

S*o this is it*, you think. You've made it. You and the other parent have come to an understanding and agreement over issues you didn't think was possible. You may be a little skeptical, even doubtful, but if all goes well, these issues are finally resolved, once and for all. Take a moment to pat yourself on the back and feel good about how far you've come in weathering the storm that appears to now be behind you, because in this chapter we are going to take the wind out of your sails.

The Fruit of Your Labors

Your agreement, as important as it might seem, is a very fleeting thing and not something that you will hold onto for very long. The words you write today may need to be changed tomorrow. The terms and understanding you have right now will need to be altered and adjusted next week, next month, or next year. To use the cliché, the only constant is change, and this will prove true throughout your co-parenting relationship.

Contrary to what you might believe, a good agreement does not prevent future disputes from turning into full-blown arguments, but a *good relationship* does. This is why there have been eight chapters dedicated to your preparation, centering, and the building of your new relationship, and only one talking about the actual agreement. Your agreement, as monumental as it is, is little more than a by-product of your new co-parenting relationship. All your preparation, your work on becoming centered and balanced in your new life, and the creation of a strong relationship have boiled down to this little and fleeting thing called an *agreement*.

This is *not* to say that an agreement is without worth. When understood properly, an agreement is valuable and crucial to the building of your co-parenting relationship. An agreement is the place where boundaries are set, expectations are defined, and the future is planned for, as far as the two of you are able. An agreement can bring order to chaos and hope to a previously hopeless situation. Attempting to co-parent without an agreement only invites disagreement, contention, and on-going conflict.

It is important to remember, though, that co-parenting agreements are not permanent. Even the best plans need continual updating and modification. Parents who lack a working co-parenting relationship will often hold tightly to past agreements—their decrees of divorce or other orders of the court—memorizing their provisions and following their direction to the letter, while life and circumstances change around them. It is common for conflicted parents to insist that they follow a parent-time schedule that was ordered when they were living only a few miles from each other, even though they now live in different states. Their previous agreement or order offers them no support or guidance. Remember that *When Forever Doesn't Last* is a book about change. To be truly effective, your agreement will also need to change as needed.

Language

Agreeing to the language of your agreement is basic to the success of any long-term resolution. Keep the words that you use positive (or at least neutral) and focused on what each of you is going to do in the future to contribute to the resolution. You may find you are agreeing to things that you have already been doing. This is okay. This is not an admission of any wrongdoing. In fact, many agreements reached in mediation look remarkably (sometimes exactly) like the order of the court that they should have been following all along. But there is a difference between voluntarily encouraging the children to call the other parent a few times during the week and being ordered to do so. The substance of your agreement or order may not change, but the relationship does. It is this new relationship that will serve the both you and your children in the months and years to come.

Keep the language of the agreement free of blame. It has not been our purpose here to teach you how to listen and negotiate tough divorce issues only to have you stuck on whose fault it is that the children haven't seen you as often as they should. Many of us want to feel vindicated that "justice was served." We want to be recognized as right, but we have seen too many parents give up the start of a good, working relationship with the other parent because their thirst for blame was just too great. Your agreement should not have any fault finding, assignment of blame, or cause of the problems that you resolved. Instead of pointing out that the other parent refused to return calls, you might say, "We have experienced a lack of productive communication." It is best to let the past remain there and look forward to a brighter future. If the other parent insists that something be said about the problems, a reframe may be useful in setting a positive (or at least a neutral) tone for the rest of the agreement.

"I" and "We" Statements

If the conflict between you and the other parent was significant, and your history has proven that the only thing you share is a lack of trust, we suggest that your written agreement use "I" statements instead of "we." Let us explain. If your agreement includes a parent-time provision that says, "We agree to have the children ready and returned on time," a violation by either parent could mean that the deal is off. If the other parent is fifteen minutes late getting the children to you, then you might feel justified in bringing them back late that same fifteen minutes. After all, they violated the terms of the agreement, so that makes it okay for you to do the same, right? "We" statements tend to be contractual and infer that people meet somewhere in the middle to resolve a conflict. If the other parent only goes partway, then permission is somehow given for you to put forth the same lack of effort and respond in kind.

"I" statements, on the other hand, clearly identify what you will do, regardless of the other parent's actions. Your compliance is not tied to anything the other parent does or doesn't do. If your agreement says, "I will return the children on time," then that is what you will do. It doesn't matter whether the other parent had the children ready on time. You said you would have them back on time, and that is just what you will do. This book is what you can do to reduce the conflict and introduce peace in your relationship. You can't control whether the other parent has the children ready on time; you can only control when you return them. Also, by refusing to play the "it's only fair" game, there is nothing for the other parent to find fault with, object to, or use as a reason to back out of the agreement. This hearkens back to the "force follows force" example we presented earlier. A relationship built on "an eye for an eye" is one destined to fail and fail miserably.

Using "I," or individual, statements makes it clear what each of you is expected to do. Spell it out. Enter into this agreement with a plain understanding of what each of you, as individuals, will do voluntarily to make this co-parenting relationship work.

Automatic "Yesses"

As we have said earlier, it is important, especially at first, to stick to the terms of your agreement. The two of you are, after all, trying to bring order and consistency out of the chaos that may have filled your life since the divorce. Strict compliance is the rule, come-hell-or-high-water. Having just said this, though, we want to remind you that life will not always go along with your best-laid plans. Opportunities and crises will insist on a change in the terms of your agreement. It is not a matter of *if* these times will arise, but *when*, and when they do, we offer two suggestions.

Keep the lines of communication open. You will probably experience many times when you or the other parent will be tempted to stray from the agreed upon or ordered parent-time schedule. If you pull up at 5:00 p.m. on Friday night, per your agreement, and you are met with a dark and empty house, or you receive a rather short voicemail from the other parent "canceling" your time with the children this weekend, it is crucial that you are open to talking about it. It does no good to become angry and accuse the other parent of willful and malicious intents, or, worse, show your disapproval of the other parent's actions by refusing to talk to him. Pause, take a moment, call him later, and listen to what the other parent has to say.

Just say "Yes." All too often parents who experience middle to high conflict after their divorce respond to requests to alter the schedule with an automatic and emphatic *no!* Regardless of the reason, this automatic refusal only fuels the fire of frustration and perpetuates the conflict. You may always be justified in saying no, but the result is still the same: trust is weakened and good faith (what little there might be) withers away and dies on the vine. We encourage you to say yes to reasonable requests, even without reasonable notice. Build this guideline right into your agreement. Unless there is a real reason to say no, agree to say yes. If the other parent calls at 3:30 p.m., says he just got basketball tickets from his boss at work, and he would like to take little Jimmy, and if Jimmy doesn't have any real plans that evening, let Jimmy go. Now, if Jimmy is supposed to practice for the school play that night, remind the other parent and apologize that Jimmy can't go but offer a willingness for next time.

If you are worried that one or both of you will take advantage of the other's good faith by making numerous requests, perhaps you could amend your agreement. Have it say that if there are more than two requests from either parent in any one month, you each agree to meet within a week to discuss it and review the schedule. Again, saying yes is not tied to the other parent saying yes, too. This is something you can do regardless of the actions, behaviors, or beliefs of the other parent. You are in control of when and how often you say yes to his requests.

Outside Support

Put simply, you have no agreement until the major players in your life have a chance to discuss it with you. The agreement is between the two of you, but it is going to take your network of family and friends to make it work. It happens too often—parents work hard in mediation and come up with a great plan, only to have a new spouse or other family member talk them out of it when they get home. The intentions of family and friends may be good, but they may not understand the amount of hard work that went into the agreement.

We encourage that you schedule time to review the terms of your agreement with your individual support systems. Like it or not, you need the support of your former wife's new husband to make your agreement work, and that might mean including him in your on-going dialogue, starting the listening process all over. And remember the mother-in-law that tormented you during your marriage? She doesn't go away with your divorce. Her influence over the other parent (her child, her flesh and blood) will continue, and you cannot ignore her influence, role, and power. If she asserts herself into your co-parenting life, you will need to blend with her energies and work toward meeting her needs (which usually consist of spending time with her grandchildren).

Parenting Plans

Many of the problems that parents experience during and after their divorce are two-fold:

1. A feeling of not being in total control of their own lives, and
2. A lack of direction and guidance—chances are they've never been divorced before.

Orders of the court contribute to both of these conflicting problems. Decrees of divorce dictate what you can and can't do but are silent on most of the day-to-day situations and troubles of co-parenting. You come to depend on these decrees as you pick up the pieces of your old life and make a new one. At the same time, however, you despise them for tying your hands and limiting your newly found freedom. This becomes especially true when you have had little input on the terms and conditions of your divorce.

It is harder to follow an order imposed on you by an attorney, a judge, or the law. In most conflicted divorces, the court does not have the time to listen to you, identify your needs, and create a tailor-made plan that is best for you and your children. You seldom get what's fair. Usually you get the law, the statutes, and very little else. You didn't agree to the terms and provisions of your decree (although you may have "gone along with it" because you had no other choice), so why should you follow it? These feelings create the desire to look for loopholes in the wording or technicalities in the statutes. For many parents, their decree or other order of the court, is insufficient to guide them as they experience the real-world difficulties of co-parenting. To provide additional structure to the new co-parenting relationship, parents and courts are turning to the use of parenting plans.

Orders of the court, by their very nature and reliance upon the law, are vague and even silent on a number of important parenting challenges and issues. They also tend to be silent on the children's needs and best interest. Instead, they focus on the parents and their legal rights and responsibilities. These are sometimes difficult to change because many cannot be amended or changed without returning to court. It is common for a decree of divorce to dedicate page after page to the division of personal and real property, but only include one paragraph about custody and parent-time. And to make matters worse, often the language of the order is not clear-cut, black-and-white instruction, but only directs the parents to agree on many issues of co-parenting. It is often this gray area that causes parents to "wing it" when unclear situations arise.

Parenting plans, on the other hand, address the big picture of your new relationship and focus on the children and how you, as parents, can meet their needs. They also usually have built-in flexibility and conditions for modification. In many states, parenting plans supplement the decree of divorce and offer parents greater control over their own lives and the lives of their children.

Parenting plans, though not a fill-in-the-blank form, are similar in content and style. As we have said before, the greater the past conflict between you and the other parent, the greater detail your parenting plan should include. Elements of a successful parenting plan will usually include:

- General parenting philosophy and religious training and expectations;
- Clearly defined decision-making abilities of each parent;
- A clear and detailed parent-time schedule, including conditions for altering the schedule, as well as who is responsible for the children's transportation;
- Child support and other financial arrangements;
- Instruction on how future problems will be addressed and resolved;
- Steps for modifying the terms of the plan.

Good parenting plans can anticipate a wide range of hypothetical situations that you, the other parent, and your children may encounter in the years that follow your divorce. The two of you are free to define your own parent-time and holiday schedules, plans for who will take care of the children when they are sick or otherwise home from school, telephone contact, and other day-to-day decisions that need to be made in raising your children. It is here that the details of *your* life are addressed and planned for. For some, your parenting plan may, in large part, mirror your decree of divorce, but it adds detail and important guidance where needed; for others it may be an entirely new document that the two of you agree to follow.

Parenting plans work well for a large majority of parents engaged in co-parenting. But some parents operate under a great deal of stress and conflict, and the thought of working out which of you is going to take the children when they wake up sick to their stomachs and can't go to school brings out a nervous laugh. For these parents, jumping right into a co-parenting plan may not be possible, or even wise. For these parents, it may be best to begin with a *parallel* parenting plan before attempting a *cooperative* one.

Parallel Parenting

In his book, *Parenting After Divorce*, Dr. Philip Stahl introduces the concept of parallel parenting and suggests its use in cases where parents of divorce find themselves in sustained levels of medium to high conflict. The term "Parallel Parenting" comes from the concept of "parallel play." It has been observed that young children, lacking the social skills and maturity of older children, tend to play side by side, in parallel. They play with the same toys, in the same room, at the same time, but they do not play together. In a similar way, some parents in a conflicted divorce may need to learn how to parent separately, or in parallel, until they develop the skills necessary to parent cooperatively.

It is a fact that some divorces are so acrimonious, where the hurt and violated trust runs so deep, that (at least for a while) are unable to communicate and otherwise deal with each other, and yet their decree of divorce requires them to discuss and "get along" on many co-parenting issues. These types of experiences are common in many divorces, and (believe it or not) are usually a transitional phase in the life of a divorce. For these parents, though, keeping apart and limiting their interaction is sometimes the best means to avoid the escalating emotions and conflict that seem to be almost automatic.

Parallel parenting plans can provide greater structure to parents who have experienced little co-parenting success. Incorporating these techniques into a plan that each of you will follow provides clear instruction on how and when you are to communicate about the children, while at the same time, it gives each of you enough space to not feel bothered or controlled by the other parent. In essence, parallel parenting means that when the children are at Dad's house, Dad's rules apply, and the same goes for Mom and her house rules. Parallel parenting means that there are few attempts to coordinate parenting rules and styles with common issues, issues such as bedtimes, acceptable foods, and movie standards. Even formal religious training is kept separate. Each parent is expected to let go of their expectations of how the other parent *should* parent the children. Those events and responsibilities that absolutely must be kept consistent between households—school and homework assignments, medication, and special developmental needs—are communicated in a simple and matter-of-fact manner, perhaps in a notebook that can be delivered back and forth.

It is important to the success of a parallel parenting plan that it be strictly followed. Flexibility, by its practical definition and design, requires both cooperation and good faith. If you are parenting in parallel, you are probably low on both. If the children's pick up time is Friday at 5:00 p.m., then you must do whatever is needed to make the exchange happen on time. It needs to be foremost on your mind all day. Work needs to be informed, and backup plans prepared in case of unforeseen complications (can a family member or neighbor pick up the children or get them ready?). When a parallel parenting plan is in place, only in the most extreme situations is it recommended that one parent call the other parent about the delay or problem. Remember, the purpose of a parallel parenting plan is to limit interaction and shut down unnecessary communication, while at the same time creating patterns of success that you can build on later.

In most cases, parallel parenting is not a permanent resolution, but a means to bridge the gulf of pain, anger, and distrust that occurs because of the separation and divorce.

Built-in Reviews

Whether you are parenting in parallel or in cooperation with each other, it is important that your agreements and parenting plans have built-in reviews. Your life during, and shortly after, your divorce will be different one, two, or ten years later. Your life, your co-parent's life, and the lives of your children are ever changing, and without a good, working relationship, many parents fail to change the agreement or order with it. When you build in periodic and situational reviews, you avoid the confusion and anxiety that usually accompany change.

So, what events or circumstances might warrant a review? Although a definitive list of divorce and co-parenting problems does not exist, some common changes tend to require significant amendments.

• *Relocation.* If one parent anticipates (or is required) to move a great distance from the other, a review of the parenting plan and parent-time schedule is in order. The decree of divorce that was entered by the court when you were living only a few miles away may have included liberal access to the children, several overnight stays, participation in school, after school, and other extracurricular activities. Now that one of you is planning or has already moved across state lines, the children will not have that level of contact with both of their parents that they have become accustomed to. It is crucial to the children's well-being that you create a new schedule that includes regular and liberal contact with the distant parent, including frequent telephone, email, snail mail, and video contact.

• *Remarriage.* When one or both of you remarry, you are, in a real sense, adding to your family. Mediation intake sessions are filled with one parent explaining that everything was going great until the co-parent's new wife or husband appeared. It is common for parents to try to ignore the new addition to the family and insist that the other parent deal with them and behave the way they used to. This is no longer the case and it is unrealistic to expect. This new spouse or significant other is now a major player in the children's lives and part of your extended, restructured family. These new spouses bring with them their own concerns, wants, and needs. Conducting a meeting with the new spouses or significant others to define and redefine roles and expectations is critical for making this transition as smooth as possible for you and your children.

• *Children's ages.* A plan and schedule that meets the needs of younger elementary-aged children will not be appropriate for when they grow older and become teenagers. Their needs, voice, and responsibilities will grow and develop as they get older. As your children grow, they will need to have a voice in what is becoming more and more *their* lives. You, as parents, will need to create a plan that sets clear boundaries and expectations from your children and also gives them room to move and live. Dating, driving, and work schedules will now need to be included and taken into consideration as you each plan time to spend with your children. Many parents, however, resist this natural evolution and demand every hour of *their* court-ordered time with the children, often blaming the other parent for not supporting them in their role as their other parent. This is not always the case, despite what it looks like. Remember, your experience is your truth and not necessarily the truth of the other parent, or your children. Build in automatic reviews when these situations arise and discuss them openly and honestly with the other parent. As your children get older (eleven or twelve years old), you may want to include them in your discussions, taking extra time to listen to their experiences, their needs, and their interests, and then work to meet them. That's your job as a parent, after all.

An Ounce of Prevention

Just as important as resolving current and possibly chronic problems with your now co-parent is taking the necessary steps to see that these problems don't happen again. For most parents, this means establishing, for the first time, a structured means of effective and on-going communication. Too often, without a way to talk about concerns with the other parent, small concerns build until one day, over what might seem like a slight provocation, tempers erupt, voices are raised, threats are made, and whatever semblance of a co-parenting relationship is shredded. Many times this happens during a location exchange, and your children are forced to watch the two people they love most screaming and yelling at each other. This is unfair and damaging to your children. Younger children will experience confusion and fear, and older children will experience resentment and anger. If you have ever been involved in such an exchange in the presence or earshot of your children, an apology to them is in order, followed by a commitment to never let it happen again.

Happily married or divorced, living across the street or across the Pacific, whether you like each other or not—parents need to communicate with each other about their children. If you are unable to do anything else together, this should be it. But what if you've tried and you can't? It may help to change your approach.

As we've said before, many of the problems and conflicts that divorced co-parents experience stem from a lack of real communication. And when they do talk, it almost exclusively consits complaints, criticisms, and other negative comments that have been bottled up over the past year. Very little dialogue goes on, while blame and finding fault are shot back and forth in some kind of verbal warfare. No one listens in spite of the volume of the argument. If this resembles your attempts to talk to your former spouse, here are some simple steps you can take to prevent them from repeating.

Agendas

Agendas are used in the business world to present problems, identify goals, guide discussion, outline steps to take, and generally see that nothing important is forgotten. The value of using an agenda, however, is not limited to the boardroom. When used regularly at a set time and date every week or month, parents who have not previously worked well with their co-parent start to effectively talk and interact with each other.

Co-parenting agendas will be almost exclusively about your children—their health, schoolwork, triumphs and challenges, and their scheduled time with each parent. To be most effective, these agendas need to be written down, perhaps in a worksheet or checklist format, and blank copies given to each parent. Communicating in this way not only ensures that the conversation stays on track, but that all of the issues that need to be addressed are covered.

As mentioned earlier, agendas don't really do much good unless they are used on a regular basis, during the good times and the bad—especially during the bad. Depending on the number and ages of your children, and taking into account your level of conflict and difficulty communicating, we suggest parents discuss items listed on the agenda at least once a week. For many parents, making an "appointment" every Sunday evening, after the children have gone to bed, to review the items on their co-parenting agenda, begins a pattern of meaningful and successful dialogue.

A written agenda also gives parents a new sense of peace during the week when issues and problems arise. If you know that you will be speaking to the other parent on Sunday, or in a week or two, you can make a note of the issue or concern on the agenda and forget about it until then. There is no need to call the other parent that instant or bring it up the next time you see her (like when you pick up the children). Agendas help the two of you talk about the right things at the right time. In short time, new and healthy patterns of successful communication will replace the old, destructive ones.

Agenda Items

Once the concept of an agenda is presented and the benefits of using it begin to outweigh your doubts, you will need to discuss and agree on what issues and items need to be included. Although each situation is different, and children and families have unique and individual needs, some topics of discussion are common to most divorced families and are included here as a guide.

- *Upcoming Parent-time Schedule.* It is important that each of you be absolutely clear on the upcoming week and month's schedule. Being clear on what days, what times, and who picks up whom and where is important to the success of your agreement. Many parent-time disputes stem from the lack of details. Who will take your oldest child to band practice? What time is Saturday's soccer match? Do each of you remember the request and agreement to trade weekends because Grandma is coming to town? This is also the time and place to tell the other parent that your boss is making everyone in accounting work extra shifts until year-end inventory is completed, and you will not be able to pick up the children until Saturday morning. Is the other parent able to take them Friday night and, if so, what time would be best to pick them up in the morning?

- *School Progress and Activities.* Many non-custodial parents feel left out when it comes to their children's education. Often they are not given copies of report cards, invited to parent-teacher conferences, or informed of special field trips or other activities their children are participating in. The agenda is the perfect place to share this part of your children's lives and make this time more meaningful for all of you. One suggestion here: take turns. Share your children's school activities with the other parent. Each of you can volunteer as a teacher's aide, take your boy to wrestling practice, and accompany the class to the zoo or museum. This is not the place to play silly games of control and revenge. Be fair. Take turns.

- *Medical and Dental Conditions.* You both care about and love your children. It is important to your co-parenting relationship that each of you is aware of the health and well-being of each of your children. Runny noses and stubbed toes may not need to be communicated as a point of concern on the agenda, but anything requiring a visit to the doctor or dentist needs to be shared and details given freely, even regular checkups. Prescriptions and other medicines need to be coordinated as the children move from house to house. If one child is ill and you have concerns about him traveling to the other parent's home, express your concern, but leave it up to the other parent whether the child comes or not. They should be given the same opportunity to exercise their role as parent and caregiver. Take time to discuss the physical well-being of each of your children. If you disagree with the doctor's diagnosis, do not take your child to another doctor to get another diagnosis or (worse) take matters into your own hands and "self-medicate" the child when he is with you. You have a duty to consult personally with your children's doctor (not a different one) and express your concerns. In the end, though, if one parent is given the legal right to decide medical treatment for your child, you may have to accept her decision and support it.

- *Special Moments and Events.* As a matter of good parenting practice, keep each other updated with special moments or achievements your children have. As a rule, anything you would include in a baby book, journal entry, or the kitchen calendar is important enough be shared with the other parent. These moments might include first teeth, potty training progress, or getting a hard-earned "A" on a test. If it brings a smile to your face, share it with the other parent. Jot it down and bring it up at your next scheduled conversation, or have the child give her other parent a call and tell him herself—sometimes good news just can't wait.

- *Reality Check-In.* It is important that parents who have a weak or struggling co-parenting relationship have a place to raise and discuss (without blame and accusation) the unusual and possibly concerning things your children say or do. We call this a child "reality check-in." If your child comes home from spending time with the other parent and mentions that he saw or did something that you feel is inappropriate, or uses a word or phrase that you think he shouldn't, it is important that you resist the urge to jump to a negative conclusion, and shovel out blame and accusations on the other parent. If it can wait, include the concern on the agenda and discuss it at your next meeting; if not, call the other parent that night after the children are asleep. How you phrase your concern, however, will determine in large part how and if it gets resolved. Begin by stating only what you know and nothing more—"Our child told me . . . Do you know anything about this?" It is important that you not accuse the other parent of wrongdoing at this stage of the discussion. Accusations are the quickest way to shut down communication and damage a relationship. Besides, you don't *know* for sure what happened. Court pleadings are filled with reports that children have come home with tales of drinking beer, watching inappropriate movies, or seeing someone naked in the shower. Most of the time these stories have rational explanations or have been otherwise innocently explained away. Remember that you are not hearing "the truth" about what happened, only your child's experience. Sometimes the reported stories or behavior come as a complete shock and concern to the other parent as well, and it may take a combined effort to give your children the care and attention they need. This keeps molehills small and manageable and helps the two of you parent more effectively.

CAUTION: If you child comes home and has been physically injured (beyond the normal bruise or scraped knee) and their explanations are less than reassuring, or a child reports inappropriate sexual touching or behavior, a report must be made to the proper child protective authorities. As hard as this phone call is, it MUST be done. They will advise you on what steps to take next, and when to speak to the other parent about your concern.

Summary

Agreements can provide structure to your life after separation and divorce, and create a foundation of consistency and successful interaction that your co-parenting relationship will be built upon. They are not, however, the end to your means. They are bridges over the gulfs that can divide and separate the two of you, when you need to be united as you support, love, and continue to raise your children. The conditions and terms of your agreement will change over time and as life moves on. Specific to your situation, parenting plans can give you greater control over your lives and at the same time provide the structure and guidance you need to figure this whole co-parenting thing out. Whether you parent in parallel or in cooperation with each other, it is important that you fulfill your obligations and responsibilities without reserve or condition. Remember, this work is about what *you* can do to make a difference for good.

More important than the written agreement is a plan to handle whatever life throws your way. Keep the lines of communication open by creating (and most important, using) written agendas until what you talk about and how you talk about it comes naturally. Open and honest communication is the key to future co-parenting success. There is no short cut or substitute. It isn't easy—if it was, everyone would be doing it. It will feel uncomfortable for a time, and you will make many mistakes along the way, but keep at it, try again, and resolve ito make this work. Your children are worth it.

Just Do It

Remember, an agreement is only as good and strong as the relationship that created it. Think of them as stepping-stones on your new journey as a divorced co-parent—not the final destination. Consider the following as you create and define the terms of your co-parenting (or parallel parenting) agreement:

1. Are you willing to fulfill your end of the bargain, even if the other parent falls short on theirs?
2. What "Automatic Yesses" can you include in your arrangement with your former spouse, especially as it affects your children?
3. Are there friends or members of your family that need to "buy off" on your agreement before they can be implemented in the "real world"?
4. Do you regularly talk to your former spouse about matters you have in common (such as the children)? Do these "talks" go well? Can you improve them in any way?

10
Children and Tribal Warfare

There is an Oriental teaching that once a person has climbed the mountain—that is, reached enlightenment—he has the solemn responsibility to return to the plains to live among the common and unenlightened masses and share his newfound knowledge and wisdom. Christianity teaches no less—"when thou art converted, strengthen thy brethren" (Luke 22:32). We are admonished to let your light so shine before men that they may see our good works and glorify the Father, who is in Heaven (Matthew 5:16). Such is our commission.

Peace is achieved one person at a time. Conversion is a personal thing. When one has found a "pearl of great price," there is an almost unconscious urge to share it with friends and family. Share the philosophy and techniques in this book with those around you, especially with your children, friends, and family members. Your co-parenting relationship not only includes you and your former spouse but also your children and extended family members.

The philosophy and techniques that you have learned here need to be shared with your loved ones and those from whom you will draw support and strength over the years. Without an understanding of what you are trying to accomplish, they won't know their roles or how to help you.

Divorce and Your Children

It is important that you recognize that the consequences of your divorce rest squarely upon your shoulders as parents. Whether you were at fault or not, or was the one who filed for the divorce, the responsibility is equally yours to help your children adjust to this frightening, and many times damaging, change that has been forced upon them. This includes the duty to resolve any differences or problems between your children and their other parent. Yes, you heard us. It is your job and obligation out of love to see that your children love, respect, and have a strong and consistent relationship with their other parent.

Your children were not the cause of your divorce nor did they ask for it (although they may have looked forward to an end to your fighting). In thinking of your children's well-being, you or the other parent might have thought it best for the two of you to separate, but it was not *because* of the children. Your decisions have uprooted their lives and upended their world. The two of you (or worse, "the Court") now tell them where they are going to live, what activities they can and cannot participate in, and when they can see their other parent—all without their permission or control. Children become the helpless victims of an adult problem, and it falls on the two of you, as their parents, to help them physically, emotionally, mentally, and spiritually cope with the loss of their old family and adjust to the new life that has been imposed on them.

A Simple Plea

As we begin speaking about the needs of children affected by divorce, we wish to share some profound words that speak to the heart of this sensitive and profoundly important subject.

"My plea—and I wish I were more eloquent in voicing it—is a plea to save the children. Too many of them walk with pain and fear, in loneliness and despair. Children need sunlight. They need happiness. They need love and nurture. They need kindness and refreshment and affection."[1]

As true as these simple words may be, regardless of circumstance or trial, they are particularly poignant when speaking about children of divorce.

Common Mistakes

Children of divorce have many needs during this difficult time in their lives. They will look to the two of you, as their parents, to meet these needs as they try to understand what is happening to and around them. They turn to you for help in identifying and expressing their feelings and to make some sense of the chaos storming around them. As parents, we do the best that we can. There are, however, some common mistakes that parents of medium to high conflict divorce often make (unknowingly) that have devastating effects on their children. A few of them are listed here, along with some practical suggestions to correcting them.

- *Confiding in your child.* Remember that it is your child who needs *your* support during this time and not the other way around. Whether you wanted the divorce or not, it is normal to experience feelings of rejection, confusion, and loneliness. It is just as normal to want to share these feelings with someone who will understand. YOUR CHILD IS NOT THAT SOMEONE. This is a frightening time for your children, and now is not the time to confide in them that you don't know how you're going to make rent this month, or respond to the latest motion filed in court, or rebuild your life again. Your children are looking to you for strength and support—they don't have enough to lend to you, although they will try. Your children need to see you as their parent, not their buddy, pal, or best friend. They need to feel that they can confide in you, expressing their fears and concerns, and that you will understand them and make things all right. Take the time to listen to them. Go out to dinner, take a picnic up the canyon, spend the day at the zoo or the children's museum, and listen to what they say. Respond and act when appropriate, but many times all they want you to do is listen, understand, and maybe give them a hug.

• *Telling your children "the truth."* Your children do not need to know "the truth" about the other parent, and the cause and details of your problems, conflict, and divorce. Let us repeat this for emphasis: Your children do NOT need to know "the truth." It is very tempting to explain to your children the real reason, you haven't seen them regularly during the past two months, which usually involves blaming the other parent. In actuality, it may be the other parent's fault that you have not seen them, but that does not give you the right to tell them so. We often hear from highly conflicted parents that the children *need* to know what a jerk (or other colorful name) the other parent is. The fact is, no, they don't. Whatever problems you have with your co-parent are yours—not your children's. The only "truth" that they need to know is that you love them and that you and the other parent are doing the best you can to work things out. Children do not need to know who is lying or keeping them from seeing their other parent or who is to blame for the divorce or the current problems. Children of divorce need to know that they are safe and that they are free to love both of their parents.

• *Not "making" them go.* Another common mistake parents make is to not "force" the children to see their other parent. This is especially common when children approach their teenage years. Too often we hear one parent say something like, "Little Jimmy doesn't want to see his dad, and I'm not going to make him. This is between him and his dad—they need to work this out," or "He's old enough to choose whether he wants to see his mother, and I'm not going to force him to do something he doesn't want to do." To this we would ask, at what point did your divorce from the other parent release you from your duties as a parent? If your child did not want to go to school, would you let him stay home and not return? Of course not. You would make him go, or better yet, try to understand their problems or hesitations about school and then, if necessary, speak to the principals and teachers and work them out. Just as dropping out of school at twelve is not an option, neither is dropping out of the other parent's life. Counseling may be needed, but just as important, the conflict between you and the other parent needs to be resolved. In the absence of open and intense conflict, children tend to cope and heal nicely.

Parents need to actively support and encourage their children to have a strong relationship with their other parent. Refusing to help the children resolve their differences with the other parent, in essence, tells them that although you have shattered their dreams for a normal, healthy, and stable family, you are not going to help them pick up the pieces. Even if you feel that you were not to blame for the divorce and separation, it is still unfair to make your *children* do the *adult* thing and work it out by themselves, without your help and support.

You may be tempted to support your child's reluctance to see, like, or love the other parent if these are your personal feelings as well. You may say that you support their relationship, or at least you won't prevent it, but do you? Again, this is where you might need to change. If you still harbor ill feelings about the other parent, return to the chapter on centering and work on it a little more. Speak to a counselor, bishop, or other trusted friend. Rise above the conflict, go to the mountain, forgive, and let it go. You can choose not to be held bound by those negative feelings and emotions. You owe it to your children, but more important, you owe it to yourself. You both love your children—do not doubt this. And as their parents, you both need to work together to help the children adjust to the reality of your divorce. This means proactively encouraging your children to love, respect, and strive for the best relationship possible with both of you. Don't abandon your children in their times of need. Speak with the other parent, talk about your concerns and the concerns of your children, and then work together to help them through this tough time in their lives. It is not their fault that they are having a difficult time adjusting to your divorce. It is not their fault that they have split loyalties and feel like they have to choose between the two of you. It is not their fault.

Family Group Conferences

One practice that is followed by many healthy families of divorce is the setting aside a regular time and place to touch base and connect as a family. Whatever you call it—Game Night, Family Night, or Special Time—a family group conference is a time to enjoy one another's company, a place to talk and be heard, and a place for you to listen. These times should be fun—play games (interactive ones, not always a video), encourage hobbies, share talents, read to them, or otherwise connect with your children. They need to know that although their family has changed, it is still a family, and can do things that normal families do.

Don't use this time to lecture, preach, or "go off" on the other parent and how bad things are. This is quality time with your children—don't ruin it by inviting hostile feelings of pain and anger. As the children feel safe again, they will begin to open up, and for you, as the parent, it is a time to listen to your children. Their comments as you play, teach, and interact with them will let you know how they are adjusting to the divorce. Your job is to listen. Many times that is all they want you do to. If you think the divorce has been hard on you, it has been devastating to your children. Having consistent family time can help calm storms in their lives, and give them a place to open up and share their feelings, and find compassion and unconditional love.

Your Children's Needs

Growing up is hard enough on children. Add divorce to their lives, and it becomes that much harder. Mix it up with pain, anger, and sustained conflict, and it is a wonder any of them survive at all. Children of divorce have very unique needs as they age and mature. Many parents, though, have a difficult time meeting these needs simply because they do not know what they are. Much of your time and resources are spent just trying to survive yourself, let alone finding the time to observe the concerns and needs of your children.

We offer here a small list of some common needs children of divorce have and how you, as co-parents, can meet them. Some of you might question why we would wait until the last chapter to include this crucial information. Why not put it first, where almost every reader will be sure to see it? The answer, of course, is that *When Forever Doesn't Last* is about changing and improving *you*. Until you are okay and have found a way to meet your own needs, you will not effectively meet the needs of someone else, including your children. Just as flight attendant instructs passengers to affix their own oxygen mask before assisting others and small children, you cannot hope to truly help your children through the effects of the divorce until you are centered, balanced, and have your own needs met. Children need strong and stable parents who will hold them and comfort them, and who will always be that sure foundation, that rock, in their lives.

So what are their needs? Every child is different, and only you as parents know what special challenges your children might face during this uneasy time in their lives. This section is in no way meant to offer therapeutic advice and is not a substitute for meeting with a counselor. There are, however, some things you can do to help your children adjust to the divorce and your new life. On the other hand, there are some things that may be beyond your abilities. If you are worried about the way your children are handling your divorce and behaving in ways that concern you, please consult a child psychologist or therapist.

For the sake of ease, we have divided children's ages into three blocks of time: infants and toddlers (ages 0–5), elementary school age (ages 6–12), and teenagers (ages 13-18). We will first give a brief and admittedly incomplete overview of what children of their age group are going through—what they are learning, what they struggle with, and generally how they are developing. Next, we will include what special needs children of divorce have and how, perhaps, to recognize these needs in your children. Last, we include some practical, simple, ways that you as parents can meet those needs.[2]

Infants and Toddlers (ages 0–5)

- *Development Overview.* These first few years are critical for children as they are laying the foundations of basic trust and relationship. The environment in which they are raised and the experiences they have with the adults that surround and care for them have a direct impact on their sense of self and trust, both in themselves and the world around them. When they reach two or three years of age, children begin to develop independence from their parents and assert themselves. Any parent who has had children of this age will attest to the "terrible twos" even if it doesn't happen exactly on cue. Children are very vulnerable at this age. A balance between structure and flexibility needs to be found and applied. As they grow older, say between the ages of four and five, their language skills seem to take off, and they become even more curious about the world around them. Making and keeping friends is important to children at this age as their interaction with others becomes more socially acceptable. They are generally a joy to be around at this age.

- *Needs.* Divorce conflict can affect children of this age in catastrophic and lasting ways, and it is important that parents understand how their fighting might be hurting their children. Even if you never speak an angry word about the other parent in the presence or earshot of your children, infants and toddlers will sense the anger and hostility in your tone of voice and body language. If you are on edge, tense, or trying desperately to curb your tongue, your young ones will experience anxiety and know that things are not right with you, and hence their world. They may withdraw and regress in their speech, potty training, and other areas of recent development. Younger children also experience a loss that is overwhelming, but that they just can't understand or express. If your children are older, they may know that their mommy and daddy are fighting, but cannot understand why. Also, it is common for children of this age to believe that they can fix their parent's problems. When they can't, this failure may have terrible effects on their newly formed self-confidence that may scar them as they grow and mature.

- *Suggestions.* Young children require consistency and routine. Stability and security is critical for their survival of the divorce. They need to know that everything is, indeed, going to be all right. Your parent-time schedule should not disrupt their routine any more than it absolutely has to. This will mean that if both parents were actively involved in the children's lives before the separation, your schedule should maintain that contact. If you have an infant (under eighteen months), frequent and shorter times are preferred and generally recommended, with few, if any, overnight stays with the other parent. Children three years and older usually have no problems going back and forth and spending the night. Children of divorce need consistent routines and rules at both houses—bedtimes, meals, discipline, sleeping habits (naps), and potty training progress. Routines need to be shared and followed in both homes. It is of utmost importance at this stage (and all stages) to keep your children isolated and free from your conflict. Never let them hear you or anyone else talk bad about their other parent. Consider this conflict poison or the plague. Never allow it to come into contact with or be exposed to your children.

School Age (ages 6–12)

- *Developmental Overview.* Children at this age are developing the social skills necessary to lead full and productive lives later on as adults. School is important as they learn about the world around them and the part they can play in it. Their minds are like sponges, soaking up as much knowledge as they possibly can. There is also a real desire to participate in outside activities such as sports, running, playing tag, and exploring the world (or open fields) around them as their imaginations are stimulated. The interests they have now will grow into the hobbies and talents they will possess for the rest of their lives. They are also maturing socially, and they begin to think beyond themselves and develop empathy. They see the effects their actions have on others. One last trademark about this age is an obsession with fairness and rules. It has been said that if you want a small pan of brownies divided up *perfectly* between four friends, give the knife to a nine-year-old. Don't even think about changing the rules in the middle of a game—your school-aged child will just not allow it.

- *Needs.* Children who experience their parent's divorce at this age sense that their family is not normal. Younger children may feel sadness and be prone to unexplained crying, while older children may respond to the divorce with anger and acting out. Children in this age group need to know that they can trust that their mother and father will make things okay. Symptoms that a child is not coping well with the divorce may include problems at school, more frequent nightmares and night waking, withdrawal (primarily in girls) and aggression (primarily in boys). Also, because of they have begun developing empathy—the ability to recognize and feel another's stress and pain—it is common for children to give their loyalty to the parent they sense is the victim of the divorce and suffering the most, and may resist or even refuse to see the other parent. Again, this attempt to take care of the parent is unhealthy and unfair to a child. They need to be kept isolated from the conflict and assured and reassured that both parents love them and are looking out for their needs. As they make more friends, allowances and flexibility in the parent-time schedule need to be made in order to support their maturing social life.

• *Suggestions.* There is a lot parents can do to help children in this age range to survive and even thrive in spite of the divorce. It is critical that maintain a consistent relationship and schedule with each parent. Remember their obsession with rules and being fair? This is not the time to play games with the parent-time schedule in some petty squabble with your former spouse. It is never okay to withhold the children's time with their other parent because they are late or behind in their child support payments. Withholding parent-time is not a card to play when you want to force the other parent's hand. For your children's sake, the parent-time schedule should be flexible and fair to handle the emergencies and opportunities that arise from time to time, but otherwise remain untouchable.

If, however, your conflict is to a level that you just can't help trading insults whenever you see each other, consider an exchange plan that limits or eliminates your contact with each other. For example, exchanges could take place at the children's school—one parent drops them off in the morning and the other picks them up and then returns them to school the next morning—or at daycare with a similar routine. If these options are not possible, make the exchange in a public place where the social pressure will help the two of you hold your tongues and keep those nasty thoughts escaping from your lips. As mentioned before, a notebook may be helpful to tell the other parent what they need to know about the children, but DO NOT use it to complain, vent, harass, or otherwise strike at each other. A note about communication: anything you need to say to the other parent should be done between the two of you directly and never through the children. You should say what you need to say in person, by phone, email, or fax. Never say to your children, "Tell your father (or mother) . . ." If, however, your child comes to you with a message from the other parent, don't take the bait and respond, "Well, you tell your father that . . ." Instead, thank the child for doing as they were asked and explain that you'll speak to their father (or mother) about it later. When you do speak to the other parent, don't come down on him for sending a message through the children. Just answer the question or address the concern and then ask them to come to you directly next time. You want him to feel comfortable in coming to you with concerns—don't scare him off by attacking his approach, regardless of how inappropriate it might have been.

Teenagers (ages 13–18)

- *Developmental Overview.* The task laid before teenagers is to create an identity separate from their parent's as they prepare for adulthood. They are becoming their own person with their own personality. To accomplish this, they will need to withdraw from their family emotionally, socially, and physically. Older than children, but not yet adults, they will challenge their parents' authority, resist suggestions for guidance, develop their own interests, and live life their way. It is normal for your sweet, giving, and obedient child to become a self-centered and stubborn teenager, seemingly overnight. It is a time of dreams of the future and goals of prosperity and love, while at the same time one of frustration and disappointment with the way things really are. If they have received the love and support from their parents and other adults in their lives, they will make good friends and grow under the light of high self-esteem and be nourished with an abundance of self-confidence.

- *Needs.* Like the rest of us, teenagers need a healthy balance between freedom and structure. Teenagers of divorce will often resist and resent being forced to share their parents, but they need to know that they are expected to maintain that connection. Having one place to call home gives teenagers greater consistency in their lives and, frankly, helps them maintain a healthy social life, as their friends will always know where to reach them. Also, most teenagers will demand that they have a say in the parent-time schedule. Although the choice should never be whether to see one parent or the other, giving them input on the details of when, where, and how can be just what they need to feel more in control of their own lives.

- *Suggestions.* One of the best things you can do for your teenager is to actively support and understand them as they create, develop, and nurture their own relationship with each parent. These relationships will look, feel, and be different from each other as your teen may look to one of you as the parent figure and the other as almost a friend or peer, preferring different activities while spending time with each of you. Different does not mean better or worse—it just means different. Remember, teenagers are trying to "find themselves" and be their own person. That is our goal as parents, isn't it? If your teen wants a voice in all this, then you'd better listen. If you and the other parent can listen at the same time, say, over dinner somewhere, so much the better. If not, jot it down on the agenda and discuss your teen's concerns, wishes, and needs at your next, regular, co-parenting meeting. Keep in mind that the choice of whether or not to see one of their parents is not theirs to make; the choice of when, what days, what times, and procedure for changing the schedule can be. Listen to your teen. When teenagers find understanding and acceptance at home, they will not be as desperate to find it somewhere else.

Keep the parent-time schedule consistent and reliable. Your teen may be planning work, dating, and other activities weeks or months out. It is not fair to change weekends at the last minute when your teen may have made other plans. As always, keep your conflict away from your teenager. It should be noted here that when your children reach these age, there is a greater temptation to confide in your teenage child and seek their comfort and understanding, perhaps even their support as you enlist them in your cause against the other parent. This was inappropriate when your children were younger, and it still is. It is unfair and unhealthy to burden a child (teenagers included) with the weight of adult problems. Even if your teen asks you about details of your conflict and problems, and you think that they are ready to hear the truth, pause before you answer. Ask yourself why your children would ask you about these things, and maybe ask clarifying questions back to discover the real reason and concerns that your teen may have.

A NOTE OF CONCERN: Perhaps more than any other age group, teenagers are at greater physical and emotional risk when exposed to their parent's divorce and conflict. Your divorce is going to be stressful on all of your children and will affect them each differently, according to their age and ability to adjust to this change. Signs that your child, especially your teenager, may not be handling the stress of divorce well might include acting out violently, withdrawal and isolation from friends and family, and may even be as severe as drug and alcohol use and suicide attempts. These are cries for help that cannot go unrecognized and unanswered. Now is not the time to determine or affix blame. If your teen is displaying any of these, or similar, behaviors, put this book down, go to the phone book if you have to, and schedule an appointment with a therapist or counselor. Answer your child's cry for help. Do not, for an instant, think that you have somehow failed as a parent if you need to call outside help. There is great strength in doing what you can and admitting to what you can't. Don't let your pride, or the way you think it might look to the other parent or to your own family, prevent you from calling in the help of a professional when such help is needed. You cannot pretend that it will all work out somehow and just go away. Your child might be strong enough to cope with and survive your conflict well enough on his own, but are you willing to risk his life on it?

As we said before, this information on your children's needs as they experience your divorce was placed at the end of this book on purpose. Only when you know what your needs are and have a plan to meet them can you stand back, go to the mountain, recognize your children's needs, see that they may be different from your own, and then take steps and make changes to meet them.

The Great Divide

Too often, divorce not only divides and separates two adults and parents, but entire families and networks of friends and associates. There is a marshalling of forces into two camps as you and your spouse prepare for the all-out war of divorce. No one actively recruits them to one side or the other—it just happens naturally. It seems that society expects divorce to be ugly. Nasty divorces make the news, are sensationalized in the tabloids, and even occasionally make the movie-of-the-week. No one talks about the majority of divorces that are resolved peacefully and on good terms. It is easy for family members to choose which side they are on, while friends and other acquaintances might need a little persuading. But in the end, parents of divorce find that they not only have each other to deal with, but the two camps that are formed—yours and theirs.

Your Camp

Your family and friends have only the best intentions at heart as they rally around you, offering support and doing what they can to help ease the pain of your divorce. They hear the stories (usually just the bad ones), see you hurt, and try to lift you up. They want to help but the trouble is that many don't know how. They tear down the other parent, pointing out all of his faults and making comments such as, "We never liked him, anyway," hoping to relieve some of the pain that you are going through. They will condemn your "ex" and tell you that you were not the one to blame. By doing this, they unconsciously make it easier for you to shrug off the role you have played in the separation and divorce and, at the same time, minimize your responsibility to work together in raising your children. They mean well, but their support sometimes makes it harder for you to begin building a working and effective co-parenting relationship with your former spouse—faults and all. If you are going to make this co-parenting relationship work, you will need the right kind of help from the right people at the right time. Although you may not control the negative feelings your family and friends may have toward your former spouse, you can do a number of things to help them give you the support you and your children *really* need.

Tell Them

Once you have become centered and balanced and are committed to a Win/Win resolution to your differences and conflicts, those around you are going to notice that you seem different. Most, we've found, won't just come out and ask about the new you, so tell them. Open up and share the new philosophy that you've adopted as your own. Explain what you are doing and that you are doing it because it is the right thing to do. Tell them how you went to the mountain, and share with them your broader vision of your role as individual and as a co-parent. You may experience some level of skepticism and doubt from those around you, but your actions and behaviors will serve as testimony to your commitment to change yourself. Don't worry if words can't express the insight that you've gained and the reasons why you feel this is the right thing to do. Share with them your plan for reaching a Win/Win resolution with your former spouse and co-parent, even if you don't know exactly how you're going to do this yet. Your goal is not to convert them to your new way of thinking but to enlist their help and support.

Don't Tell Them

You may not be able to control your family's reactions to your divorce, but you can control *what* you tell them and *how*. Your family may not need to know every little detail, complaint, and struggle that you go through. Your family is almost certain to feel protective and worry about you. Some may even feel the need to "do something" about it. If you have a brother who has a short fuse and considers it a matter of honor to punish your ex for what he has done, the best way (maybe the only way) to prevent him from doing something that you will both regret later may be not to give all the details. If it upsets your parents to see their own flesh and blood suffering, it may be best not to tell them everything. Tell them about your accomplishments and the good things that are happening to you and the children, and perhaps include how they can better help you and the children during this time of your life.

What You Don't Need

You may not know exactly what kind of support you need, especially in the early stages of the divorce. It is, however, easier to recognize the type of support that is damaging to your future co-parenting relationship and that runs contrary to the healing principles taught here. Common forms of negative support include verbal attacks and cuts against your ex; contacting him without your knowledge to express their feelings about him; threatening or warning him to stay away and never hurt you again; making it difficult for the other parent to see or spend quality time with the children; calling him names or spreading rumors about him; and driving by his house several times at 11:00 p.m., to name only a few. This type of behavior, as you well know, does more damage to your already strained relationship.

As uncomfortable as it will be, you need to be direct and firm with your family and friends. You may need to remind them that this is *your* divorce, not theirs. Blend with the energy of their good intentions and let them know that, although you appreciate their efforts, some of their specific actions and behaviors do not support your new desires and goals. What you *do* need is for them to find ways to lift you up without tearing the other parent down. You might suggest that you could use their help watching or picking up the children when you're running late from work, or otherwise being available to help you meet your co-parenting obligations.

Sometimes you just need someone to listen to your struggles and fears without fanning the dying embers of your divorce into another raging inferno. What you need is a friend (maybe from work) who will listen to your problems, nod from time to time, support the way you are feeling, then buy you a Diet Coke, and change the subject to a less emotional one, like the weather or sports. Be specific in what you do and do not need, giving them suggestions and direction, and your family and friends will not let you down.

A Double-Edged Sword

There is one instruction that you must be absolutely clear on with members of your camp: you consider any negative comment about the other parent a direct attack on your children. Make it clear that you will not tolerate any of them to bad-mouth your children's other parent in any way or at any time in your presence or within the walls of their own home. Your children must never be exposed to this insidious brand of poison. Make no mistake, negative words, labels, and comments are poisonous! They slowly eat away at and kill a child's identity and sense of worth. Whatever opinions your friends and family may have, they need to keep to themselves. Your children are, after all, part you and part the other parent.

Children are very sensitive to the world around them—especially to their parents—during and shortly after a divorce. What they don't hear directly (when you think they're not listening or won't understand), they pick up in your tone and body language, and when they hear that their mother or father is irresponsible, a liar, and can never be trusted, they will begin to wonder if they are that way too. Explain this to your friends and family. If you have to, make it a rule or condition that they will have to meet in order to see your children. Protect your children from this subtle but corrosive venom.

Their Camp

If you got along well with the members of your spouse's family when you were married, don't be surprised if you are now suddenly public enemy number one. As hard as this might be, try not to take it personally and return the favor by cutting them off too. Your former spouse's family will display fierce loyalty to their own flesh and blood, just as yours does to you. It doesn't matter if the other parent had the affair, or was the abuser, or walked out on the marriage, or otherwise caused the divorce. Don't expect any sympathy, compassion, or cooperation from them any time soon.

If members of the other parent's family *are* sympathetic to your situation and can see that you are doing what is right and best for their kin and the children, your task of building a better co-parenting relationship can be much easier. Just as with your own family and friends, tell them what you want to do and the steps you are taking to do it. Give them instruction (if they ask) on what you need from them and how they can help. Let them know that you will not allow them to degrade the other parent or cut them down. As good and justified as it might make you feel to know that members of your ex's family are on your side, you are not preparing for battle or trying to prove that you are the better parent—you are seeking peace and a working co-parenting relationship. When they become convinced of your sincerity and commitment to a mutual beneficial outcome for you, the children, and the other parent, they will be eager to help. Keep in mind that working with and through these other family members is not a substitute for working directly with your children's other parent.

Summary

You and your children will have many needs as your family changes with divorce. Some of your needs will be similar, but many will be different. As parents, your children will look to both of you to identify their feelings, make sense of their rapidly changing world, and give them the tools and support they need to survive your divorce. Knowing the unique and special needs that children of divorce commonly have will enable you to spot the signs of stress your own children may be showing, and you can get them the help they need. Your friends and family will play a big role in your success as a divorced co-parent. Help them understand what you need them to do and give them instructions on how to help you, so they can see how they can become an even greater support. With all of you working together, you and your children can survive and even thrive in spite of the divorce.

Just Do It

This might be a hard chapter to take in. It may be apparent that some of your own actions have caused unnecessary stress on your children. To this we say, forgive yourself and begin today to make life a little easier and healthier for your children. Take some time to reflect on the following questions. Be honest with yourself. Your answers—and your commitment to them—may help lay the foundation of your future co-parenting arrangement.

1. Have you ever confided "adult" topics in your children?
2. Do you have a healthy support system of family or friends?
3. Have your children seen a therapist or counselor since the separation or divorce? Have you consulted with them as to their needs and how to meet them?
4. Have you recruited family or friends into your camp?
5. Have you given them specific direction to help you and your children adjust and deal with the divorce?

NOTES

1. Gordon B. Hinkley, "Save the Children," *Ensign*, Nov. 1994.

2. One of the best and thorough references touching on the needs of children of divorce is the book, *Parenting After Divorce*, by Dr. Philip Stahl. If you have any questions about your own children's behaviors and needs, this is an excellent resource and place to start.

Conclusion

We began this journey by claiming that *When Forever Doesn't Last* was a book about managing the change called divorce. Divorce changes you, your spouse, your children, your family, and your friends. It also changes your hopes, desires, goals, and what you can and cannot do with the rest of your life. These changes do not have to be negative, viewed as restrictive, or something you despise and resent. Divorce can be a new beginning, a chance to start over, a way to learn from past mistakes and better yourself, and help you find greater joy and satisfaction out of life. For most, the blessings are not easily seen nor do they come without some hard work and struggle, but the blessings are yours if you will take them.

The more you understand this change and its effects on you and your life, the better equipped you will be to blend with its energy and redirect it to yours and your children's benefit. Fight against it, and you will injure yourself, the other parent, and even your children. *When Forever Doesn't Last* can help you manage the many changes brought on by divorce, especially as it affects you, your perspective, your goals, your approach in dealing with problems, and, most important, your new relationship with your former spouse and now co-parent to your children. Let's review how.

A Change in You. There is only one person in the world that you can change and control, and that is you. Hard as you might try, you will be unable to truly change anyone else. Oh, sure, you might force someone into action by applying pressure or threats, but they will resist your efforts and strike back at the first opportunity. People—me, you, your former spouse, and everyone else—do things for one of two reasons: because we want to, or because we are afraid of the consequences of not doing them. The first will bring about real change, the other an unnatural and strained compliance. Divorce court is filled with cases where one or both parents are fighting to control the way the other parent spends their time with, interacts, treats, and raises the children. There is great power in knowing what you can and cannot do. Make a list of those things that you have no control over. By doing so, you create another list of those things you can control. Making a change in your thoughts, words, and actions will change the nature of the relationship, which will change the outcome. All this you can do without input, permission, or support from your former spouse. You may not be able to control the circumstances or what happens to you, but you can always choose your attitude and your response. Don't let anyone tell you different.

A Change in Perspective. Not all conflicts are contests. A conflict needs a resolution, while a contest produces a winner and by its very nature, a loser. The sooner you can shed the Win/Lose expectations of your divorce, the sooner you will be able to identify your needs, find similar needs in your former spouse and children, and then work toward meeting them. When it comes right down to it, divorce is little more than a restructuring of the family. The two of you will always be parents, even though you are no longer husband and wife. Court has a tendency to turn the conflict that needs to be resolved (so the you can begin to heal and pick up the pieces of your former life) into a contest that pits you against the other parent in some kind of battle. Whether the two of you walk away from the marriage as friends, or battle it out with your dying breath before a judge, in the end the two of you are expected to work together as co-parents to raise and parent your children. Divorce is not a contest or battle to be won; it is a new relationship that is created.

A Change in Goals. Divorce is not about getting revenge, punishing, or proving anything to other parent, nor is it to win at all costs. When divorce is no longer a contest (in fact, it never was), the goals you set become those of mutual benefit, cooperation, trust, flexibility, compassion, forgiveness, empathy, resolving concerns, and meeting needs. You no longer have the expectation to separate and never see the other parent again; instead, you work to lay the foundation of a healthy co-parenting relationship, finding a way to work together despite your differences. Once you have become centered and balanced in your own life, you can then make it easier for the other parent to follow your example and enjoy the same peace that you have. Also, yours is the task of helping your children cope and adjust to the divorce that has changed their lives so much. This is a frightening time for children of every age, and every effort should be made to listen to their concerns, comfort their fears, and provide consistency and a sense of security.

A Change in Approach. Force follows force. The harder you push and force your will upon the other parent, the more resistance you will experience and the harder he will push back. It is not usually important who is right or wrong, whose fault it is, or who is the strongest and has the most resources to get what they want. It *is* important to create a plan for the future that is clear and will prevent further misunderstandings and conflict. The best communicators are the best listeners. The other parent will not want to, or even be able to, listen to your needs and concerns until you first understand his. All too often, divorced parents spend too much time talking and trying to convince the other parent of one thing or another, and not enough time listening. Using the principle of flow, or blending, you can set aside your own needs, wants, and concerns for a moment or two, and listen to the other parent first. Once she feels understood, she lets down her defenses and is more willing to understand what your needs are. This listening first and talking later is unnatural to most of us, but this approach is the surest way to get dialogue going again. Realize that there is no conflict too great for you to resolve.

A Change in Relationship. Divorce changes the definition and nature of your relationship with your spouse. The court is very skilled at dissolving your roles as husband and wife, but is ill-equipped to create your new roles as co-parents. There are those surrounding you to help you in this monumental task such as family members, friends, attorneys, guardians ad litem, therapists, and mediators, but in the end, it is your responsibility to forge a new relationship with your former spouse. If you see yourselves as enemies until the day you die, you may wage war with your ex for years until you can't remember what you started fighting about. The pain, injury, and suffering that you hold on to and refuse to release are like poisons traveling slowly through your entire system until they reach your heart. If, however, you can see that your roles as father and mother have not been erased, but only changed due to the divorce, you can see yourselves as partners who share common interests, love, and goals with respect to your children. It took the two of you to create your children, and it will take the two of you to help them through this divorce and this change.

You have been given the task and responsibility to work together to effectively raise your children as divorced co-parents. "Impossible!" you say. You were unable to work together and communicate when you were married. Do we expect you to start now? To this we, and your children, say, "Yes." Whatever differences the two of you have in values, goals, beliefs, and parenting styles must now be talked about openly and honestly. A parenting plan must be created that resolves concerns and meets your and your children's needs.

This will not be easy. You will need to prepare yourself physically, mentally, emotionally, and spiritually to accept the challenge that lies before you. You will need to find your center and become balanced in your new life as a divorced parent. This center and balance point must be something that is yours to control and that cannot be taken away. From this center you will gain great strength and balance to let go of the past and face whatever the future brings.

There is no quick fix to building an effective co-parenting relationship with your former spouse. The skills and techniques presented here are not tricks to manipulate the other parent into doing or giving you what you want. Not all techniques and suggestions will work in your case. You may have to modify some to fit your circumstances and create entirely new ones to meet your needs. You will make mistakes along the way and will need to apologize to your children and their other parent more than once. You will need to forgive, as well as ask for forgiveness. You will need to be humble enough to make the first move and strong enough do the right thing.

It is our goal and hope that in reading *When Forever Doesn't Last*, you will be better equipped to respond to the conflict and struggles of co-parenting after divorce in a way that encourages honest discussion, dialogue, cooperation, and mutual benefit. It will not be easy. It may always prove to be a struggle. But if you keep at it, making every move from your center of strength, you will improve the nature and outcome of your relationship with the other parent. Give you and your children the gifts you will all value above all else—a life without the heavy burden of conflict, the freedom to live and love, and the peaceful assurance that all can and will be well.

Appendix 1:

The "Charitable Divorce"
Advice for Those Who Counsel

W e, the authors, present this last section with a great deal of care and trepidation. It is not our intent to tell you what you may or may not be doing correctly when a member of your ward family experiences divorce. Rather, we offer a new or different perspective on divorce and the role we each have, especially as Church leaders, to truly help those we have a stewardship over.

Spiritually Balanced

If you have read *When Forever Doesn't Last*, then you have, at least, some degree of understanding of how divorce affects family members. Those who experience divorce are often desperate and seek out advice wherever they can. Too often this advice is destructive and serves to perpetuate the conflict. Any contention is of the adversary, and it may fall on you, and you alone, to help your ward member stay spiritually balanced during this challenging and painful time in his life. You must be diligent and proactive in your efforts to urge the member not to abandon the Christlike principles and values that you, and others, have tried to teach and instill upon him over the years. When the going gets tough, you need to stand ready to help support the entire, the *eternal*, family as it is being restructured during this act we call divorce.

Parents and children of divorce have specific needs that only you (and perhaps the other parent's leader) can meet. We touched on this earlier but it bears repeating here. Consider the words of Helaman 5:12:

> And now, my sons, remember, remember that it is upon the rock of our Redeemer, who is Christ, the Son of God, that ye must build your foundation; that when the devil shall send forth his mighty winds, yea,

his shafts in the whirlwind, yea, when all his hail and his mighty storm shall beat upon you, it shall have no power over you to drag you down to the gulf of misery and endless wo, because of the rock upon which you are built, which is a sure foundation, a foundation whereon if men build they cannot fail.

Divorce is a raging storm and whirlwind, and make no mistake: the devil preys upon our members during this time in their lives, and he desires to drag them down to the gulf of misery and endless wo. When we side with the mother or father who lives within our ward boundaries, we often unintentionally help create and sustain the conflict that is their "mighty storm." For example, it was common in the authors' experience to see motions for contempt filed in District Court alleging that a custodial mother had her child "secretly" baptized (or blessed or ordained) by a grandfather or (worse) the new step-father, instead of the non-custodial father. In most cases, the leader permitted the ordinance to take place without ever contacting or meeting with the other parent. Actions like these only serve to strengthen the adversary's mighty winds and sharpen his shafts in the whirlwind.

Consider another example of the "injustice" many non-custodial parents have expressed over the years: the interview for a temple recommend includes a question to make sure financial obligations are being met, but no such question is directed at the custodial parent to ensure that visitation and parent-time is being regularly offered and followed. You might be hesitant to get involved. You may just want the courts to handle these and other matters. However, in this hectic and frenzied time of these members' lives, your influence, steady hand, and counsel may be needed now more than ever. In fact, you may be the only hope of keeping the *family* intact while the *marriage* falls apart.

> You may be the only hope of keeping the *family* intact while the *marriage* falls apart.

Might we suggest ways here in which you might help your members withstand this storm and remain strong on the foundation, the Rock, which is a life centered in the principles and teachings of Jesus Christ.

The Charitable Divorce

Jesus Christ is the only one who can heal the broken heart and bind up their wounds (Psalm 147:3). It will likely fall on you to keep the members centered and focused on Jesus Christ. Help them to not abandon the eternal principles that Jesus taught when they are faced with the terrifying change and pain that divorce brings. To aid you in this daunting task, we offer the "Charitable

Divorce," inspired by Moroni 7:45, by which you might better help the members remain strong and firm in their faith and testimony.

Charity

- **Suffereth Long:** This is a trying time for those who experience divorce. Sometimes, the parents believe that the conflict, problems, fighting, anger, and pain will just never end. Encourage them to stay strong and be patient. There is a window of time after the divorce is final (usually about two years) when parents and children alike are trying to pick up the pieces of their lives to reassemble them in a way that works for them, making many mistakes along the way. This is an especially trying time if the parents are not engaged in mediation or conflict coaching. It is during this time that they are forced to learn how to communicate (effectively) with one another, and work with each other as they co-parent their children. Most times there is no way to "short-cut" this adjustment period, but mediation and counseling or therapy can help.

- **Is Kind:** Divorce is a time of terrible and very real mental, emotional, and physical pain. It can be hard to show kindness to anyone during this time, especially a former spouse who has caused such pain. It will help the parents heal if they can at least be kind in their actions: saying "yes" to additional parent-time (visitation), sending copies of good report cards without being forced to by the court, encouraging the children to call, write, or otherwise build a healthy relationship with the other parent, and so on. Often these "small and simple things" can bring big things to pass.

- **Envieth Not:** It is common for each divorced parent to view the other as the one that "has it easy." One parent might envy the other's free time, affluence, greater support system, or time spent with the children. Envy will lead to a sense of it being unfair, and legal (or other) actions are sometimes taken to even the playing field. Behaving in this manner can only increase the levels of conflict. If they are grateful for the blessings that they do have, the feelings of pain and loss for the things they don't have will diminish and healing will begin to take place.

- **Is Not Puffed Up:** No one wants to believe that the divorce was his or her fault. Even men and women who have broken sacred marital and temple covenants will find a way to blame the divorce on the other parent. This desire to *be right* often gets in the way of *doing the right* thing and seeking a resolution to their conflict. Humility is the great protector. Help them resist the temptation of being prideful and puffed up in their own self-righteousness.

- **Seeketh Not His Own:** Often divorced parents will seek and envy those things that are not theirs. Sometimes they will even try to sabotage the other's happiness and future relationships in an attempt to keep things fair.

Misery begets misery, force begets force, and in the end, everyone is hurt by such actions.

- **Is Not Easily Provoked:** It is common for mediators and other conflict resolution professionals to refer to high conflict families as fragile. If parents are not standing firm on that sure foundation, they are off balance and will not withstand the storm raging around them. They are easily and often provoked by the words and actions of the other parent, quick to retaliate and respond "in kind." Help them remain calm when such situations arise. Encourage them to communicate with the other parent and work things out, instead of going to court or taking matters into their own hands.

- **Thinketh No Evil:** It is too common with all of us to assume the worst in someone when things go wrong and conflict arises. This is especially true during a divorce. Parents make accusations and emphasize only the bad in each other in attempts to "win" court hearings. Harboring ill thoughts for the other parent prevents them from forgiving and being healed by the One who can heal. All of your conversations with the parents should be positive, uplifting, and looking out for their *eternal* family.

- **Rejoiceth Not in Iniquity:** As we just mentioned, parents experiencing a contested or otherwise troubled divorce may find pleasure in the misfortunes of their former spouses. They may even take steps to *cause* these misfortunes. In their every action, parents should be Christlike and forgiving.

- **Rejoiceth in Truth:** Divorced parents often do not want to hear that the other parent is adjusting to the separation, or that the children actually (and still) *like and love* the other parent. They may not want to hear that he got a promotion at work (unless it means going back to court for more child support), or that he has found someone new in his life. If she is unhappy at the happiness of the other parent, or the children, she is not centered or balanced in her own life. Help her to forgive the other parent and forever shed the chains that bind her down.

- **Beareth All Things:** There are times when one parent will be forced to bear more than his fair share of the divorce load. One parent may not be able or willing to work cooperatively with the other or is constantly calling to cancel parent-time or other activities. One parent may be ready and willing to let the problems of the past remain there, while the other can't seem to let them go. One parent may be called on to be strong and do more than the other for a while. This is common. Empathize with the parent, support him with what he needs, but don't agree with him that other parent is "no good" or "doesn't care about the children"—this will only perpetuate the problems.

- **Believeth All Things:** Parents going through a difficult divorce will often doubt what they have been taught and have believed for years. Their dreams for a happy and eternal family may be shattered, as might be their faith and trust in others. They may doubt their own worth and give up. Don't let them. The pain and loss that divorce brings can be made right again, but only as they exercise faith and remain close to Him who can "bind up their wounds."

• **Hopeth All Things:** Hope is often the first casualty of the divorce. Parents are in the middle of the raging storm, trying not to get knocked off that Rock by the shafts in the whirlwind. They can begin to think that there is no hope for happiness or peace. Again, this is not true! Hope is sometimes the only thing that will help them keep going: hope that someday the fighting will stop, that the pain will go away, that they will be happy again, that they can forgive, and be forgiven. It is this hope that will carry them through the worst of times.

• **Endureth All Things:** This last element of charity encompasses all that we have discussed here. Divorce is difficult for everyone involved: mother, father, children, extended family, friends, and neighbors. The parents will have to endure the consequences and life changes brought about by divorce, but they need not endure it alone. God has promised mercy to those who are merciful, comfort to those who mourn, and peace to those who seek it, but they cannot find this rest except they forgive and apply the attributes of charity, for "charity is the pure love of Christ, and it endureth forever, and whoso is possessed of it at the last day, it shall be well with him" (Moroni 7:47).

As Church leaders, you are called to do a great work. This work is not easy, and it often involves "reproving betimes with sharpness, when moved upon by the Holy Ghost: and then showing for afterwards an increase of love" (D&C 121:43). The struggling and angry custodial parent in your ward may not like what you have to say about the upcoming baptism of her child, but it is your responsibility to help all of the family (whether they all live in your ward, or not) to stay spiritually balanced. Support their *eternal* family and help them obtain the peace and healing that will strengthen them and bring them closer to God.

Appendix 2:

Mediation Frequently Asked Questions

Q: What kind of cases can be mediated?
A: Most types of disputes and legal actions can be effectively mediated, particularly in situations where emotions run high and where relationships are involved, such as divorce, paternity, probate, neighborhood and family disputes.

Q: How long does mediation take?
A: Depending on the number and complexity of the issues, mediation can be concluded in as little as one or two sessions.

Q: How much does mediation cost?
A: Mediation generally costs parties about ¼ of what an attorney would charge.

Q: Is the mediator our judge?
A: No. The mediator is a trained, professional, and neutral party to the conflict. A mediator's job is to help facilitate an agreement, not to decide the issues.

Q: How can I find a good mediator?
A: There are a few national mediation associations, many of them focusing on divorce and domestic mediation. Many state court systems have a list, or roster, of certified and approved mediators. Whenever possible, ask potential mediators for client references.

Q: Do I need to select a mediator that shares my religious faith?
A: No. Where the mediator is not a judge or decision-maker, it is not

important that he or she understand the details of your religious issues as long as you and your former spouse do. Sometimes, however, parties are more comfortable with a mediator that has a personal understanding of their faith and issues.

Q: If I choose mediation, will I still need a lawyer?

A: You may still need to contact an attorney even if you reach agreement in mediation. The role of mediator is separate and distinct from that of a lawyer. A lawyer may still be needed to draft any legal documents to file with the court and finalize the divorce. However, this fee should be very low (a few hundred dollars vs. tens of thousands each for litigating the divorce). After all, you did all the hard work in mediation.

Q: What is the difference between mediation and arbitration?

A: Mediation is the process of using a neutral third-party to help facilitate the negotiation and resolution process. The mediator is not a judge and cannot make decisions for the parties.

Arbitration is the process where a neutral third-party hears the facts of the case and attempts to help the parties reach an agreement. However, if they are unable to do so, the arbiter is appointed by the courts to render a decision that can be either binding (final) or non-binding. Arbiters are subject-matter experts and often attorneys or former judges.

Q: When is the best time to begin mediation?

A: Any time is a good time to begin the resolution process. Of course, the sooner you can mediate your dispute, the sooner you can reach an agreement and begin picking up the pieces, so to speak, of your life.

Q: What if we can't agree in mediation?

A: If no resolution is reached in mediation, the parties are free to pursue their matter in court, or some other conflict resolution process. Usually, though, many of the issues in dispute are resolved in mediation, leaving only a few to be decided by a judge. This can dramatically reduce the amount of legal and court fees.

Q: Is mediation legally binding?

A: Mediation is generally not binding. An agreement, called a Memorandum of Understanding, is generally considered "an agreement entered into without the advice of legal counsel" and not enforceable by itself in court. However, parties with attorneys present at the mediation can agree to be legally bound by the agreement.

Q: What are the advantages of mediation over litigation?

A: Mediation leaves you in control of the outcome.

It's quicker than litigation.

Fees are substantially less.

Your relationship is preserved.

You get a chance to express and discuss what is most important to you

The mediation is confidential

Q: I want to use mediation, but the other side doesn't. What can I do?

A: This is very common. Often when one parent suggests mediation, the other is suspicious and automatically says no. Some mediators will send an introduction letter, sharing the mediator's experience, neutrality, and an overview of the process, usually at no charge. Also, giving the other parent a list of three or four mediators to choose from can lessen their apprehension about the process.

Appendix 3:

Resources

There are many local and national resources to help ease the stress and conflict parents experience while going through a divorce. To better help our readers, church leaders, and concerned family and friends, please visit our website below for an updated and current list of these resources, as well as general information about mediation and conflict resolution.

The Association of Mormon Mediators
www.mormonmediators.org

Suggested Reading

Many books are available that touch on the principles presented in this book. Of course, in offering a suggested reading list, we want to encourage you to continue (or start!) reading the scriptures. It is here, in these holy and inspired words that the Lord, the One who knows *exactly* what you are going through and what you need, can speak directly to your soul.

Having said that, there are good books out there that offer sound and practical counsel and advice to help you in your journey to heal and find peace both during and after your divorce. We offer a few of our favorites here. An updated list may be found at www.mormonmediators.org.

Attitude of Gratitude, M. J. Ryan (Conari Press, 1999)
The Magic of Conflict, Thomas F. Crum (Touchstone, 1998)
Aikido in Everyday Life, Terry Dobson and Victor Miller (North Atlantic Books, 1994)
The Seven Habits of Highly Effective Families, Stephen R. Covey (St. Martin's Griffin, 1997)

The Co-Parenting Survival Guide, Elizabeth Thayer and Jeffrey Zimmerman (New Harbinger Publications, 2001)

Emotional Intelligence, Daniel Goleman (Bantam, 1995)

Parenting After Divorce, Philip Stahl (Impact Publishers, 2000)

Why Marriages Succeed or Fail, John Gottman (Simon & Schuster, 1995)

Getting to Yes, Fisher, Ury, and Patton (Penguin Books, 1991)

Getting Past No, William Ury (Bantam, 1993)

Getting Together, Roger Fisher and Scott Brown (Penguin, 1989)

Man's Search for Meaning, Victor Frankl (Beacon Press, 2006)

Crucial Conversations, Patterson, Grenny, McMillan, and Switzler (McGraw-Hill, 2002)

About the Authors

Guy M. Galli is a veteran of the Utah Judicial system, a divorce and child custody mediator, and the former Director of the State of Utah, Third District Court, Co-Parenting Mediation Program. An instructional designer and corporate trainer, he is also the author of the LDS bestselling novels, *Lifted Up* and *Shadow Hunter*.

David C. Pruden founded the Family Mediation Center of Utah in 1991, and has been practicing ever since. An author and speaker on subjects related to various aspects of adult and adolescent development, he has been an instructor in the department of Family and Human Development at Utah State University. David is also a life member of the National Academy of Family Mediators and a member of the Association of Mormon Counselors and Psychotherapists (AMCAP).